The CONESTOGA RIVER
A History

DONALD KAUTZ

FOREWORD BY STEVEN NOLT

The History Press

Published by The History Press
Charleston, SC
www.historypress.com

Copyright © 2021 by Donald Kautz
All rights reserved

Back cover, top image, courtesy of LancasterHistory.
All photography is by the author unless otherwise noted.

First published 2021

ISBN 9781540246530

Library of Congress Control Number: 2020948440

Notice: The information in this book is true and complete to the best of our knowledge. It is offered without guarantee on the part of the author or The History Press. The author and The History Press disclaim all liability in connection with the use of this book.

All rights reserved. No part of this book may be reproduced or transmitted in any form whatsoever without prior written permission from the publisher except in the case of brief quotations embodied in critical articles and reviews.

How sweet it is, when gloaming tide
Concludes a sultry summer's day,
By some cool water's shaded side
With loved ones, young or old, to stray!
And where did any eye survey
A landscape matching scene on scene
Where Conestoga winds its way
Betwixt its trees and meadows green?
O, lovely Conestoga!

—*James D. Law, 1903*

CONTENTS

Foreword, by Steven M. Nolt   7
Preface   9
Introduction   11

1. Fur, Fin and Forest   19
2. Wagons, Forges and Farms   33
3. Slack-Water Navigation   44
4. Bridges and Mills   68
5. Steam and Electricity   90
6. Conservation   101
7. Twentieth-Century Struggles   113
8. Parks and Recreation   120

Appendix A. Timeline   135
Appendix B. Bridges   141
Appendix C. Mills   145
Appendix D. Floods   149

Notes   153
Sources   157
About the Author   160

FOREWORD

"You cannot step twice into the same river," the Greek philosopher Heraclitus observed two and half millennia ago. This observation, which at first glance appears to accent transformation—the river does not remain the same, nor does the one entering the water—actually points to a more complex relationship between change and continuity. After all, change is a constant according to Heraclitus, and the maxim itself has had the sort of staying power that finds us still musing on its meaning centuries later.

Whether stepping into the Conestoga River for the first time or for the hundredth, one discovers in this southeastern Pennsylvania watercourse the dynamic interplay of continuity and change across time and place. In this lively story of the Conestoga, Donald Kautz explores these undercurrents chronologically and topically.

The river has been a constant source of food and sheer survival for both animals and humans, even as the species and people in its watershed have changed. It has been a place of relaxation and reflection for those gathered on its banks or floating on its current, and it has been a site of conflict and controversy as people argued over ownership and even over its designation as a creek or a river.

As the chapters that follow attest, the Conestoga has done many different things. It brought neighbors together around mills and forges, and it kept them apart until bridges spanned its channel. In some cases, the river offered to unite people in shared recreation, only to have the powers that be insist on separation and segregation.

Foreword

Over time, the Conestoga has witnessed human efforts to effect dramatic changes in the landscape. Clearing forests, draining wetlands and cultivating farm fields, as well as constructing towns and villages, altered the river's watershed in significant ways. And yet, just as profoundly, the river's resiliency resisted the proclamations and plans of those who stood along its banks. When, in the nineteenth century, people created a system of slackwater dams that promised to transform the river into a series of connected ponds—a fascinating story of engineering and investment—the river yielded for a time, but the fury of floods and the persistent flow of water eventually triumphed, and the river, as a river, returned.

In some cases, humans have worked in concert with the river's remarkable impulse toward regeneration and renewal. Following decades of dumping sewage into the waterway, concerned residents formed the Lancaster Conservancy and, with other groups, worked to restore the Conestoga and to help the river's interrelated ecosystems to rebound.

In fact, the river's testimony to the interconnectedness of life and to the necessary relationship between continuity and change may be one of its greatest, if underappreciated, gifts. William Cronon, a historian of nature and the environment, has noted that contemporary Americans often seem blind to the things that bind them to the landscape and to one another, separating city from country, pavement from plowed field, headwaters from confluences. As a result, "the stories we tell about the journeys we take in life," Cronon observes, stories of movement from "country to city, young to old, innocent to corrupt," have a way of solidifying those divisions and hindering us from reflecting "on how tightly bound together [we] really are."[1] Maybe the antidote to this affliction of isolation is a trip down the Conestoga, attuned to its connecting the habitats, communities and livelihoods of its valley in subtle and profound ways.

We can't step twice into the same river, but perhaps the river can teach us a vital lesson we need to learn over and over again.

—Steven M. Nolt, Elizabethtown College

PREFACE

The concept for this book came about in several phases. It began with photography. I decided that I would explore the Conestoga River photographically, primarily as fine art photographs of scenes along the river. My goal was to publish some of those images in a coffee table book that I could make available to friends and relatives. I blogged about the project as it progressed, mainly to help organize the material. I started in the headwaters and worked my way down the river. When I got to the lower part of the river, I began to discover the remnants of the old locks and dams that were part of the Conestoga Navigation System. My blog post on this topic attracted the attention of Benton Webber, a Lancaster Township engineer, who also had an interest in exploring the story of slack-water navigation on the Conestoga River. Ben asked me if I would be interested in collaborating with him on the topic, and I agreed, which led to a period of researching old documents and hiking to the locations of the locks to observe and photograph any artifacts we found there.

My blog also attracted the attention of Phil Gerber, president of the Millersville Area Historical Society, who asked me if I would be willing to give a presentation about the Conestoga Navigation at one of the society's meetings. I quickly recruited Ben Webber to be a co-presenter, and together we created a presentation of the information we had gathered, illustrated with a slideshow of my photography. So many people showed up for the first presentation that they had to turn people away. Since that time, Ben and I have given the presentation at many locations around the county. It

Preface

was at one of those presentations that Ken Hoak from the Conestoga Area Historical Society came up to me afterward and said, "Someone should write a book about this." I took his subtle suggestion and wrote down what I had learned about the Conestoga Navigation Company. You will find that material presented in the chapter on slack-water navigation. One chapter does not make a book, however, so at the suggestion of my publisher, I expanded the work to include the entire river.

INTRODUCTION

The Conestoga River meanders for about sixty miles through the fertile farmlands of Lancaster County in southeastern Pennsylvania until it empties into the Susquehanna River. The Conestoga watershed drains approximately 217 square miles. The area is part of the Pennsylvania Piedmont lowlands. This area was once covered with a shallow sea. Various species of shellfish lived and died in the sea, their discarded shells building up to create great sheets of limestone. Eventually, tectonic forces pushed up to form the Appalachian Mountains. Over time, these mountains eroded, forming deep, rich soil in the alluvial valleys. This, in turn, enabled great forests to grow, and the forests provided the habitat for abundant wildlife. Bear, deer, elk, foxes, otters, raccoons, wildcats, wolves and the much-coveted beaver, not to mention many species of birds and waterfowl, all made their home in the forests and wetlands of the Conestoga Valley.

The first Paleo-Indians began to arrive in the area between twenty thousand and twelve thousand years ago. At that time, until the arrival of European settlers in the eighteenth century, the Conestoga Valley was much different than it is today. The valley was more like a swamp than the single channel that we now know. The valley was made up of numerous, interconnected streams that flowed around islands of vegetation. The system was resistant to flooding because the floodplains were broad and marshy, and the underlying soil was porous. The historic floodplain was full of vegetation with root systems that held the soils in place even during

INTRODUCTION

high water flow. The Conestoga has an inverted stream profile. This means that unlike most rivers that have their steepest slopes in the headwaters and level off as they approach their mouths, the Conestoga starts out with gentle slopes that increase as it approaches the Susquehanna.

Where is the source of the Conestoga River? The subject of where the river begins is more controversial than it would seem it should be. Some writers seemed to be insulted if the Conestoga did not begin in Lancaster County, as if the river needed to be bound to municipal boundaries laid out by the British. The other problem for assigning a specific location for the start of the river is how you determine when enough of the springs and rivulets have coalesced together to form a main channel. And when does a "creek" become large enough to earn the label "river"? But the Conestoga predates the British occupation and does not care about municipal jurisdiction. Nor is the river concerned with the need to denote a precise beginning, so we must be content to be a little ambiguous when defining the source of the river.

The headwaters of the Conestoga are made up of two branches. The West Branch begins in a marshy area of the Pennsylvania State Games Lands #52 north of the Pennsylvania Turnpike, northeast of Morgantown. The East Branch begins somewhere just north of Elverson. The two branches join at a point along Mill Road just south of Morgantown. For all practical purposes, this spot where the two branches join marks the beginning of the Conestoga.

The Conestoga and its sister stream the Pequea Creek form a double watershed system. The Conestoga and Pequea with their tributaries drain most of what is today Lancaster County. I prefer to use the word "drain" instead of "watered," as in "the Conestoga Valley is watered by the Conestoga River." The "watered by" phrase obscures the actual workings of hydrology. The valley is watered by the precipitation that falls on it in the form of rain or snow. Excess water that the land cannot readily absorb makes its way to the lower ground where the river flows. So, I believe it is more accurate to say that the land waters the river. When you see a fertile valley with a river flowing through it, the river is not watering the valley; rather, the presence of the river indicates that the valley is well watered. Such is the case with the Conestoga Valley.

The principal tributaries of the Conestoga are the Muddy Creek, Cocalico Creek, the Lititz Run, the Mill Creek and the Little Conestoga. The Muddy Creek begins in Berks County and flows about twelve miles until it joins the Conestoga near Hinkletown. The Little Muddy Creek and the Black Creek are the major tributaries feeding the Muddy Creek. The Muddy Creek watershed is mostly composed of agriculture and forest

Introduction

The East and West Branch join to form the main channel near Morgantown.

land. The Cocalico Creek flows through Ephrata Borough and joins the Conestoga near Talmage. The major tributaries of the Cocalico are the Hammer Creek and the Middle Creek, which flows out of the Middle Creek Wildlife Management Area. The Cocalico watershed is predominantly agricultural except for the Ephrata Borough. The Lititz Run begins near the town of Lititz and joins the Conestoga at Pinetown near the village of Oregon. The Santo Domingo Creek is the major tributary of the Lititz Run. The Lititz Run watershed is mostly agricultural but is heavily developed in the town of Lititz.

The next major tributary of the Conestoga is the Mill Creek, which joins the Conestoga just below the city of Lancaster. The Mill Creek watershed is composed of a mix of agricultural, forested and developed land, with about three-quarters being agricultural. The Mill Creek has one of the highest dairy cow densities in Pennsylvania. The Little Conestoga Creek originates near Manheim and flows west of Lancaster and Millersville and joins the Conestoga below Rock Hill. The West Branch of the Little Conestoga forms its major tributary. About half of the Little Conestoga watershed is agricultural, with some densely populated areas near the middle section.

INTRODUCTION

TABLE 1. TRIBUTARIES

Tributary	Township	Coordinates
Cedar Creek	East Earl Township	40.138708, -76.026664
Muddy Creek	East Earl Township	40.152521, -76.116490
Groff Creek	West Earl Township	40.115214, -76.217836
Cocalico Creek	West Earl Township	40.114995, -76.226536
Lititz Run	Manheim Township	40.105349, -76.248661
Mill Creek	West Lampeter Township	40.001542, -76.304515
Little Conestoga	Manor Township	39.951173, -76.368734

Is the Conestoga a creek or a river? The portion of the Conestoga upstream from the city of Lancaster is consistently referred to as a creek, while the lower part of the Conestoga is called either "creek" or "river" depending on the goals of the writer. The map prepared in 1824 by the engineer Captain Ephraim Beach for the Conestoga Navigation proposal clearly labels it as the "Conestogo River." Frank R. Diffenderfer (1833–1921), who was an associate editor of the *Lancaster New Era* newspaper and one of the founders of the Lancaster County Historical Society, wrote an impassioned plea on behalf of the Conestoga River. Here is an excerpt from his "Plea for the Conestoga River" that was read before the Lancaster Historical Society in 1912:

> *Pennsylvania is one of the best-watered states on the American continent. There are, perhaps, a thousand streams within her borders which, in any European country, would be called rivers, while not even a baker's dozen of them are spoken of as rivers here at home.*
>
> *I shall not make my appeal to sentiment only, but to what the verdict of the past 5000 years has been. I shall show you that some of the greatest events of all time have occurred on the banks of streams no larger, nor as large as the Conestoga, and that their names have come down to us in song and story, linked with the heroic deeds of the ages.*
>
> *The number of its affluents, large and small, is from two to four hundred. To ask us to call such a stream a creek, is a proposition that offends human intelligence.*
>
> *One of the most beautiful streams in the world flows quietly through the green meadows and along the sunny braes of Lancaster County for a*

Introduction

Cattle graze near the headwaters of the Conestoga River.

> *distance of more than sixty miles, draining a territory 315 square miles in area, affording endless themes of beauty to the brush of the painter and the fancy of the poet.*
>
> *It is the Conestoga "Creek" to most of our people "and it is nothing more"; yet it is a river, just as truly as are some of the most noted streams of the world which have been called rivers for thousands of years.*
>
> *Our Conestoga has borne its present misnomer long enough. Let no member of this Society ever again speak or write about it as a "creek." Call it what it really is, and what it deserves to be called—The CONESTOGA RIVER.*

The Conestoga was officially designated a "river" in 1973. Diffenderfer's plea inspired the American poet Lloyd Mifflin to write the following sonnet for the Conestoga River:

> "CONESTOGA RIVER NEAR LANCASTER IN JUNE"
> *Within the shadow which the foliage throws*
> *The browsing cattle by the waters dream;*
> *The white arms of the trees above thee gleam;*
> *And on thy slopes the ripening harvest glows.*

Introduction

From the meadows of the hay the fragrance blows
Sweeter than all Arabia!...What a theme
For revery thou art, O pastoral stream,
Idyllic in thy beauty and repose.
Nine arches hath thy Bridge of classic mould
One for each Muse clear mirrored on thy breast;
Amid this quiet of the evening hours
Tranquil thou flowest toward yon waste of gold,
Where, shadowed 'gainst the fulgence of the West,
The stately College lifts her clustered towers.

The spelling of the name "Conestoga" changed over time. The earliest references used a spelling ending in "oe." As an example, here is an excerpt from an ode written as part of the dedication of Franklin College in 1787:

Hail, ye banks of Conestogoe!
Fertile, favor'd Region, hail!
Chosen seat of FRANKLIN COLLEGE,
What but good can here prevail!
Science never comes alone,
Peace and Plenty,
Heaven itself support her Cause!

By the middle of the nineteenth century, the "e" had been dropped, and the name became "Conestogo." The first engineering map of the proposed Conestogo Navigation System uses the label "Conestogo River." There is a Conestogo River in Waterloo, Ontario, that was named by Mennonite settlers who moved to Canada from the Lancaster area in the early 1800s. Apparently, they brought with them the spelling that was in use at that time. Eventually, the name changed again to the form ending in "a." In this book, I mostly use the current spelling, except in a few cases where the context requires an older spelling.

The history of the Conestoga River watershed could end up being a history of Lancaster County. That topic has been covered already by professional historians, so I saw no need for me to take that approach. How should one approach a book about a river? Should I take a topical approach? Or perhaps my narrative should follow the flow of the river? In the end, I decided to take a chronological approach and write it from the point of view of the river. What things happened along the river and what effect did they

Introduction

have on the river? The organization of this book is generally chronological, although, as you will see, many of the topics overlap one another. You may also notice an ecological theme winding its way throughout the narrative.

I hope you enjoy the story that unfolds on the following pages, and I hope you catch a glimpse of what a beautiful asset the Conestoga is to those of us who live in Lancaster County. I have lived in the Conestoga Valley all my life, and I know that it is easy to pass over its bridges without paying any attention to the river, except when it floods and blocks our way. After reading this book, I hope you will join me in appreciating this local treasure and take the time to stop and visit one of the many parks and trails along its banks or enjoy a lazy summer afternoon paddling a canoe or kayak down the stream.

Chapter 1

FUR, FIN AND FOREST

For thousands of years before the first Europeans explored the New World, the forests of North America were occupied by the various tribes of aboriginal people. These peoples were mostly nomadic and would move from place to place depending on the availability of game and fish. For about 2,500 years, the area was inhabited by a group of people known today as the Shenks Ferry Native Americans. They disappeared around AD 1550. By the time the first Europeans began to arrive, the area was occupied by many diverse groups. It is difficult to sift through the many names that are mentioned in the history books. As the people traveled from place to place, they often took the name of the place where they settled. For example, the people living along the Piscataway Creek were called Piscataways until they migrated to Pennsylvania, where they were known as the Conoy. Further complicating things is that various European settlers transliterated the tribal names into their own vernacular. The league of nations was called Five Nations by the English and Iroquois by the French. What follows is an attempt to catalogue the main tribes that had some influence in the Conestoga watershed.

THE FIVE NATIONS (IROQUOIS)

In the Northeast, in what is now New York and Canada, was the area occupied by the Onondagas, Oneidas, Mohawks, Cayugas and Senecas.

Sometime in approximately the mid-1400s, the five groups formed a league of nations called the Haudenosaunee or "People of the Longhouse." The league was governed by a council of fifty chiefs; however, the league was egalitarian. Each tribe in the league maintained its own language and territory, and none was superior to the others. The French referred to the Haudenosaunee as the Iroquois League and the British called them the Five Nations. In 1722, refuges from the Tuscarora tribe joined the league, after which it was called the Six Nations. The head village, or capital if you will, of the Haudenosaunee was at Onondaga, just south of Syracuse, New York, on today's map.

THE DELAWARE (LENAPE)

Along the eastern seaboard of New Jersey and eastern Pennsylvania lived the Leni Lenape people. The Leni Lenape were made up of groups of related clans with similar languages. The two primary languages were Unami and Munsee. The Lenape were matrilineal, meaning that they reckoned their lineage through their mother's kin. When a couple married, they would live with the wife's family. When the English settled the area, they named the river after the first governor of Virginia, Thomas West, Third Baron De Le Warr. The English called the Lenape living along the river the Delawares. In 1624, when the Dutch founded their colony called New Amsterdam, the Lenape began selling furs to the Dutch, primarily beaver pelts. This began the lucrative fur-trading business that unfortunately led to the overharvesting and near extinction of beavers in the Delaware Valley.

The English colony of Pennsylvania was founded in 1682 by William Penn. Penn made a treaty with the Lenape under the famous tree at Shackamaxon in which Penn and the leader of the Lenape, Tamanend, agreed to live together in peace for as long as the rivers run. William Penn advocated a policy of benevolence with the Lenape, although his growing colony eventually put pressure on the Native settlement and hunting grounds. William Penn's sons did not follow their father's policy and employed various schemes to subsume the land of the Lenape. During the French and Indian War, the Lenape sided with the French, partly due to a promise that their land would be restored. After the war, many of the Lenape migrated west to the Ohio Valley, although a few remained.

A HISTORY

THE SHAWNEE (PIQUAWS, PEQUEA, SHAWANESE)

The Shawnee seem to have originated in the Ohio Valley but occupied most of what later became Pennsylvania and Virginia. The Shawnee were related to the Lenape and called the Delawares their "grandfathers." In 1698, some sixty Shawnee families from Georgia applied to the Susquehannocks for permission to settle near the Pequea Creek. The name of their town was Pequehan. Their principal chief was named Opessah. They remained there about thirty-four years. Opessah was chief until 1711, when he abdicated and Lakundawanna was elected his successor. They began migrating to Ohio around 1728 and had all moved out of Lancaster County by the middle of the eighteenth century.

Frenchman Martin Chartiere lived with the Shawanese at Pequea and married an Indian woman. Several years before his death in 1708, he moved his trading post to a point about a mile above the Conestogas' fort in Manor Township. His son, Peter Chartiere, also married a Shawnee woman and later convinced the Shawnee to fight with the French in the war of 1755–58. In 1709, the governor of Pennsylvania came to Pequehan and offered each of the Shawanese braves a gun if they would join in an expedition about to start against the French in Canada. The Shawanese declined the offer, not wanting to get involved in a conflict where they would likely not prevail.

THE CONOY (CONOISE, GAWANESE, GANOWESE, PISCATAWAY)

The Conoy were originally settled along the Piscataway Creek near the Potomac River. The tribe was a tributary to the Five Nations who used the Piscataway settlement as a stopping point on their southern expeditions. For this reason, fearing that the Virginians would take up arms against them, the tribe requested permission to move farther north. In 1704, William Penn welcomed them to his province. They settled for a while along the Susquehanna at a place called Conejohela, which was located at present-day Long Level in York County. Later, they crossed the river and settled along the Conoy Creek. In 1722, their main settlement was called Conoytown in what is now Donegal Township, Lancaster County. The Conoy remained in that area until about 1744, when, feeling crowded out by settlers, they moved north near Shamokin.

The Conestoga River

THE SUSQUEHANNOCKS (MINGOES, MINQUAYS, CONESTOGOS)

For the purposes of this book, the principal focus will be on the Susquehannocks, later known as the Conestogos. The Susquehannocks spoke the Iroquoian language and were possibly related to the northern tribes. When Captain Newport set sail for the New World on the *Discovery*, *Susan Constant* and *Godspeed* to form the settlement at Jamestown, the Susquehannocks occupied a town with a stockaded fort on the Susquehanna River at the foot of Turkey Hill in what would later become Manor Township. At their peak, they could field six hundred warriors from their stockade at Turkey Hill.

In the summer of 1608, Captain John Smith left Jamestown and sailed up the eastern shore of the Chesapeake Bay on an exploratory mission. At the head of the bay, he encountered a hunting party of Susquehannocks. Captain Smith described them as more muscular and larger in stature than other Natives he had seen. Smith said:

> *They seemed like giants, and were the strangest people in all these countries, both in language and attire; their language well becomes their proportions, sounding from them as a voice in a vault. Their attire is the skins of bears and wolves, some have cassocks made of bears' heads, and skins that a man's head goes through the skin's neck, and the ears of the bear fastened to his shoulder, the nose and teeth hanging down his breast, another bear's face split behind him, and at the end of the nose hung a paw, the half-sleeves coming to the elbows, where the neck of bears and the arms through the mouth, with paws hanging at their noses. One had the head of a wolf hanging in a chain for a jewel, his tobacco-pipe, three quarters of a yard long, prettily carved, with a bird, a deer, or some such device at the great end sufficient to beat out one's brains, with bows, arrows, and clubs suitable to their greatness.*[2]

Historians had assumed that Captain Smith was exaggerating, but years later, when a bridge across the Octorara Creek was being constructed as part of the Columbia and Port Deposit Railroad, some human skeletons were found that were larger than usual in size. Also, bones excavated near the Susquehannock stockade not far from Washington Boro indicated that they were people of above average height. It should be noted, however, that the average height of a European male in Smith's day was around five feet, seven inches.

A History

Left: Susquehannock by Captain John Smith. *Ellis and Evans.*

Below: A Native American longhouse.

The Conestoga River

In 1658, a group of English Quakers led by Josiah Cole explored the wilderness along the Susquehanna looking for a place where the Friends could settle peacefully. They visited the Susquehannocks at their village, where they were received courteously and where they "entertained us in their huts with much respect."[3] When Cole returned home and reported his findings to the others, they were greatly impressed and asked Cole to go back and ask the Susquehannocks if they could purchase some of their land. However, by the time Cole returned in 1660, the Susquehannocks were too busy with their war against their northern neighbors to negotiate with the Quakers.

On December 19, 1656, the Dutch West India Company of Amsterdam required the Senecas (that is, the Five Nations) in New York to bring their furs to the Delaware River instead of the Hudson. This was done as a convenience to the Dutch shipping. However, the route to the Delaware meant that the Senecas needed to travel through Susquehannock territory. This led to heated intertribal conflicts. In the early 1660s, the Senecas made their way south as far as the head of the Chesapeake Bay, where they fought against the Susquehannocks in what was known as the Beaver Wars and terrorized the English settlers in that area. In June 1666, several of the Susquehannock leaders appeared before the Maryland Council that met at St. John's in St. Mary's County. They warned the council that the Senecas planned to attack the Marylanders' fort in August of that year. The Maryland Council organized an expedition to march against the Senecas, but those in the expedition got cold feet and returned without engaging their enemy. The Senecas did not appear in August but did attack the following spring. In August 1667, the Susquehannocks again sent for assistance and ammunition to fight the Senecas. The Marylanders promised to do so but never actually sent any assistance up the river, leaving the Susquehannocks to battle the Senecas on their own.

The situation continued to worsen during the following years, finally prompting the Marylanders to appoint another officer to command their troops. They selected Colonel Ninian Beale. Beale marched his forces up the east side of the Susquehanna to the fort at Turkey Hill. There, he reportedly gave the Five Nations a blow from which they did not recover. The exact date of this battle at the fort is hard to pin down but would have been between 1667 and 1682. The ranks of the Susquehannocks were severely decimated at this time, and they no longer held the importance that they once commanded.

During the seventeenth century continuing into the eighteenth, the fur trade was big business among the Swedish, Dutch, French and English traders. The Susquehanna River was a major thoroughfare for the movement of skins and supplies. The Susquehanna and Schuylkill canoe path ran from the Susquehanna up the Conestoga following the East Branch. From there, the goods moved over a short portage over to the Pine Creek, down the French Creek to the Schuylkill and on to Philadelphia and the Delaware. (I am using the present-day names of the water courses; they did not carry those names back then.) Thousands of beaver pelts were transported by the Susquehannocks along this route.[4] The fur traders were an adventurous lot, rugged outdoorsmen who spent half their time bartering with the Natives in the wilderness and the other half bartering with the European settlers who wanted their goods. In many cases, the first white people with whom the Natives came into close contact were the fur traders. Their impression of white people was often formed by these encounters. Most of the traders in the area that would later become Lancaster County were based along the Susquehanna and along the Conoy Creek. One of the prominent traders of the time was a French Canadian named Peter Bazaillon. Another French trader named James Le Tort lived in the area for a time. A village west of Millersville still bears his name.

A pair of Quakers, Edmund Cartlidge and his brother John, set up a trading business along the Conestoga. Edmund settled near the mouth of the Conestoga and John settled a few miles to the east. Edmund served as justice of the peace for a few years. In the winter of 1722, the brothers traveled to Maryland to do some trading and visited a Seneca named Sawantaeny along the Monocacy River. They entertained the Native with rum in the evening and sat down to do business the next morning. During negotiations, Sawantaeny got angry when he thought that he was being short-changed. A scuffle broke out, and Sawantaeny went into his cabin and came out with a gun. Edmund wrenched the gun from the Native's hand and struck him on the head with the gun so hard that it shattered the wooden stock. The Cartlidge brothers then packed up and rode off, leaving Sawantaeny to die in his cabin. At first, the Cartlidge brothers fabricated a story that the drunken savage had attacked them and they accidentally killed him in the struggle to get control of the gun. But when word of the murder reached Philadelphia, the governor was concerned that this affair would jeopardize trade with the Five Nations. So the governor sent James Logan and Colonel John French to Conestoga to investigate the matter. On March 14, Logan and French were joined by Peter Bizaillon and a large company of Delaware, Shawnee, Conoy and Conestoga leaders. After a slow day of testimony (the talks had to be translated from English to Delaware and from Delaware to Iroquois and Shawnee), Logan was able to defuse the situation by proposing to send a delegation to the Iroquois with gifts of consolation and by arresting John and Edmund Cartlidge and taking them to jail in Philadelphia. In August, Governor Keith went to Albany with a delegation of colonists and Indian representatives and was able to finally lay the matter to rest. The Iroquois then urged the governor to release the Cartlidges from prison. "One life is enough to be lost," they said. By fall, the brothers were back in their homes on the Conestoga.[5] This affair damaged their reputation somewhat, but nevertheless they remained on the Conestoga for about twenty years.

WILLIAM PENN

On May 4, 1681, King Charles II granted a charter to William Penn for a large portion of land west of the Delaware River. Penn named the land Pennsylvania and established its primary city on the Delaware. He called this the city of brotherly love, Philadelphia. In 1683, Penn visited the Susquehannocks at their fort. How could he explain to them that his king over the sea had granted to him ownership of their territory? Penn was careful not to offend the Natives but was also not tolerant of them quarreling among themselves. Soon after this, the remnant left their fort on the river shore and moved to their town on Turkey Hill about four miles farther up the hill. Once established at this new location, they became known as the Conestogoes. *Conestogoe* in the Native tongue is generally believed to have meant "people of the cabin pole." Here Penn granted them five hundred acres of land that became known as "the manor"; today, it is Manor Township.

Penn was forced to return to London to defend his interests against Lord Baltimore. He remained in London for some time, even spending some time in debtor's prison. In 1701, Penn returned to the manor again, where he showed the Conestogoes a parchment that had been signed by two Indian "kings" granting to him the rights of ownership to the Conestogoes' land on both sides of the Susquehanna. It turned out, however, that the two "kings" were members of the Delaware tribe. When the Conestogoes, not surprisingly, expressed dismay at this, Penn placed the document on the ground and assured them that he would hold their land in common with them. He told them that they "should be esteemed by him as his people, as the same flesh and blood with the Christians, and the same as if one man's body was to be divided into two parts."[6] Then he gave them the parchment and told them to preserve it for three generations as a witness of this council to their children.

In 1706, a group of Quakers visited Indian Town and asked permission to hold a "religious service." The Conestogoes sought council from an elderly woman named Conguegas who was sometimes referred to by whites as their "queen." It turned out that three days earlier, Conguegas had a dream in which she found herself in London, where she met William Penn. Penn told her in her dream that he would soon come to them to preach. So, satisfied that this was fulfillment of her dream, she consented to allow the Quakers to hold their service. The Quaker preacher, Thomas Chalkley, preached to them about "faith in Christ." The Natives showed their agreement, especially when he talked about "the light in the soul."[7]

In the spring of 1711, seven "mennonist" families from the Palatinate region of Germany settled in the Pequea valley just south of the Conestogo River. The first tracts of land were allocated to Martin Kendig, Wendel Bauman, Hans Funk, Christian Herr, Hans Herr, Martin Meilin and Jacob Miller. The land purchased by these first German immigrants stretched from present-day Strasburg to Willow Street. The influx of new immigrants led to the formation of a new township in 1712. The new township was named Conestogoe. The land was mostly forested with heavy timber consisting of oak and hickory. The Germans recognized that the large trees meant that there was rich soil beneath and were not deterred by the amount of hard work it would take to clear the land. In 1717, another larger group of Mennonite families arrived and purchased land adjacent to the first group. The Germans cleared the land and added to their farms a little more acreage each year. They built log cabins at first and later were able to build houses from stone. Christian Herr built his house in 1719. This house, named for Christian's father, Hans Herr, is the oldest surviving house in Lancaster County. The house served as a Mennonite meetinghouse prior to the American Revolution. Today, the Hans Herr house is open to the public as a museum.

It was not long until these new settlers were building mills on the Pequea and the Mill Creek. One of the first mills on the Conestogo was a log gristmill built by Theodorus Eby in 1718. Eby's mill was located somewhere along the river across from the present-day Sunnyside peninsula. Another early mill on the Conestogo was a fulling mill built in 1728 by Stephen Atkinson. It was located south of what would later become the borough of Lancaster. The first dam at this mill was torn down by inhabitants farther upriver because

THE CONESTOGA RIVER

The Hans Herr house, built in 1719 by Christian Herr, served as an early Mennonite meetinghouse.

they claimed it severely reduced their supply of fish. The dam was rebuilt with a fish ladder in place to allow the fish to migrate upstream.

In 1728, the English residents of this part of what was then western Chester County began lobbying the government to form a new county. The primary reason was the great distance (nearly one hundred miles) to the county seat. They also cited the lack of adequate bridges as one of the reasons for erecting a new county with its seat of government closer to the residents. The council in Philadelphia agreed, and on May 10, 1729, the new county was formed out of the part of Chester County that lay north of the Octoraro Creek. The new county was called Lancaster after commissioner John Wright's ancestral home in Lancashire, England.

Eight magistrates were appointed, and these men immediately called a public meeting of prominent citizens to agree on the names of the townships and fix their boundaries. This first magistrates' court met on June 9, 1729, at the tavern of John Postlethwait in Conestogoe Township, not far from the Conestogo River. After working out the names and locations of the seventeen townships, the magistrates had to decide on a location for the county seat. Several locations were presented for consideration, one being Postlethwait's tavern where the magistrates were already meeting;

another was Commissioner John Wright's ferry town on the Susquehanna (present-day Columbia). The residents of the eastern part of the county wanted a location that was more central, so the magistrates located a plot of land about eight miles east of Postlethwait's about a mile north of the Conestogo where there was an inn kept by George Gibson next to a spring and a hickory tree. At first, the magistrates believed that the lot they had chosen had not been surveyed and therefore belonged to the Penns. The provincial prothonotary, Andrew Hamilton, was asked to do a title search. Hamilton discovered that the lot had been awarded to a Richard Wooler of London, who was now deceased. Hamilton then asked his agent in London to purchase the lot for himself.[8] The elder Hamilton soon after transferred the property to his son James. James Hamilton sold three lots of land to the county: one for the courthouse, one for the county prison and one for a market. Hamilton's town, originally called Hickory Town, was named Lancaster after it became the county seat.

Between the new town of Lancaster and the Conestogo River was a large wetland called the Dark Hazel Swamp. A small stream ran out through the town into the swamp. The stream was later called Roaring Brook. This stream has been completely covered over but still runs under present-day Water Street.

FRENCH AND INDIAN WAR

In May 1754, Colonel George Washington led a band of Virginia troops against a group of Frenchmen and Indians at Laurel Hill, Pennsylvania, thus bringing the war between the French and the English into the colonies. It is beyond the scope of this book to tell much about this conflict except to say that many of the Shawanese and Delawares joined the French against the English, partly on a vague promise that if they succeeded, the French would return to them the lands they had sold to the English. The Natives under the command of the French terrorized the white settlements along the upper Susquehanna. On October 16, 1755, a band of Delawares attacked a settlement along Penn's Creek (present-day Selinsgrove), killing fourteen settlers and capturing eleven. By the end of October, the French and Indian forces were within five miles of Harris' Ferry (Harrisburg), prompting John Harris of Paxtang to write a letter to Edward Shippen of Lancaster in which he stated:

The Conestoga River

The Indians is cutting us off every day, and I had a certain account [from Andrew Montour] *of about fifteen hundred Indians beside French being on their march against us and Virginia, and now close to our borders, their Scouts Scalping our Families on our Frontiers daily....I am informed that a French officer was expected at Shamokin this week with a party of Delawares and Shawanese, no doubt to take possession of our River; and as to the state of the Susquehannah Indians, a great part of them is actually in the French Interest.*[9]

The Conestogos had become extremely destitute by this time. Many of them had little clothes to wear. It was no longer safe for them to go out hunting for food, so they went from farm to farm begging for food or bartering for it with reed baskets and brooms. Alcoholism was rampant. James Wright of Columbia was appointed by the governor to supply them with clothing and food to keep them from freezing or starving.

When the white inhabitants of the upper Susquehanna, having fled their homes, came into Lancaster County and Philadelphia, the suspicions against the Conestogos grew with each new story of the atrocities that were committed upriver. The French and Indian War ended in 1760, but an uprising by Chief Pontiac in 1763 caused animosities to rise again against the small tribe. On December 13, 1763, a company of Scots-Irish men from Paxtang, Hanover and Donegal headed to Conestogo Indian Town to destroy the place and its people. Early the next morning, they attacked the town, killed and scalped its inhabitants and burned the town. There were only seven persons in the town on that morning, as most of the tribe were spending the night elsewhere. One of the men who was slaughtered that day was an elderly man named Sheehays who was a boy when William Penn visited in 1701 and who still had the parchment that Penn had charged them to preserve. A boy named Tong-quas, or Chrisly, escaped and alerted the manager of the tragedy. When the remaining Conestogos returned to find their homes destroyed and their family and friends dead, they did not know what to do, as they had nowhere to go. They also feared that whoever did this atrocity would return for them as well. The Lancaster authorities told the fourteen survivors to go to Lancaster, where they would be housed in the city workhouse for their protection. But then, on December 27, about fifty or sixty men armed with rifles and tomahawks appeared suddenly in the town at about two o'clock in the afternoon, stabled their horses at the White Swan hotel on the square and walked the block down King Street to Prince Street, where they broke

A History

This marker indicates the approximate location of the Conestoga Indian Town.

into the workhouse and killed the fourteen Conestogos in the yard. The workhouse was located beside the old jail where the Fulton Theatre stands today. The city magistrates were attending a Christmas service at St. James during this time, and by the time they could be notified of the violence taking place across town, the "Paxton Boys," as they were later called, had remounted their horses and ridden out of town.[10]

There were at least two Conestogos who survived the massacre. There was a couple whose Christianized names were Michael and Mary who lived in a hut on the property of a Mennonite farmer named Christian Hershey. When the Paxton boys came into the area looking for the Conestogos, Michael and Mary hid in the Hersheys' basement. Michael and Mary survived into their eighties and were buried on the Hershey Homestead, now part of Kreider Dairy Farms in Manheim. The Conestogo tribe is gone, but their memory remains in the river that bears their name.

Chapter 2

WAGONS, FORGES AND FARMS

Lancaster County continued to grow in population at a prodigious rate. Twelve years after James Hamilton began laying out lots in Lancaster, there were approximately 270 houses and close to 750 residents. This inspired the Hamiltons to request a borough charter from the governor. The charter was granted on May 1, 1742.[11] As the city grew, it became necessary to drain the many swamps and wetlands within the city limits. Stone sewers were constructed to carry the excess water down to Roaring Brook. This increased the flow down Water Street, into the Dark Hazel Swamp and eventually into the river. Meanwhile, the German Mennonite immigrants from the Palatinate continued to pour into the region, settling all along the Conestoga and its tributaries. Year after year, the German farmers cleared the forest and enlarged their farms. As the trees were cleared to make way for agriculture, the runoff into the river increased dramatically. The effects were gradual at first and were hardly noticed by the new settlers who had other matters to occupy their minds. But the pressure on the river's ecosystem had begun.

An increasing population generates pressure for better modes of transportation. One of the first roads was the Great Conestoga Road that ran from the Conestoga Indian Town past Postlethwait's tavern through Lampeter, Strasburg and Gap into Chester County and on to Philadelphia. This road was in use as early as 1712 but by 1730 was already in a state of disrepair. In that year, the citizens petitioned for the road to be rebuilt. But since the town of Lancaster was now the county seat, and Postlethwait's was no longer of great importance, the road was laid from Lancaster to Philadelphia. The principal roads in colonial times were called King's Highways and were laid out by the governor. The new road ran from the Conestoga east of Lancaster to Compassville on the dividing line between Lancaster and Chester Counties. This was known as the Old Philadelphia Road and was probably the most important road in the county for the next sixty years. The highway was extended to Wright's Ferry in 1734.

Around this time, the German farmers began to build a heavy wagon designed for hauling freight. The wagons were made of wood, but they were not flat. Instead, the bodies curved up on each end to keep the freight from shifting as the wagon traveled. The wagons could carry about six tons of goods and were covered with white canvas covers to protect the contents from the elements. Each wagon was pulled by four to six strong horses and could travel about twelve to fourteen miles per day. These wagons, of course, were called Conestoga wagons and were the primary freight hauler in the late eighteenth into the early nineteenth centuries.

By 1750, there were as many as ten thousand of these freight carriers, principally used to carry farm produce into Philadelphia. First-class teams would customarily carry bells on the horses: five small bells on the lead horses, four larger bells on the middle horses and three even larger bells on the pole horses. The three sizes of bells not only warned travelers on the road ahead that a large wagon was approaching but also made music as

A Conestoga wagon in Lancaster (postcard). *Author's collection.*

the horses moved. In some parts of the country, there was a custom that if a wagon got stuck or could not negotiate a hill and another teamster had to help pull them out, the assisting teamster would take the bells of the troubled team. When a team arrived at its destination without its bells, it meant they had trouble on the road. This gave rise to the saying "I'll be there with bells on."[12] The brake handle on the Conestoga was on the left side of the wagon, requiring the teamster to walk on that side or sometimes ride the rear horse on the left side. When two wagons met going in opposite directions, they would pass on the right so that the drivers would have the best visibility. This is likely what gave rise to the American practice of driving on the right side of the road.

The Conestoga wagon drivers were known for enjoying a cigar as they traveled along the road. The drivers' salary did not enable them to be able to afford the more expensive cigars that their customers preferred, so they smoked long, thin, cheap cigars made in Conestoga. The name of these cigars got shortened to "Stogie." Eventually, the term "stogie" applied to any brand of cheap cigar.

IRON FORGES

In 1718, a man named John Jenkins requested and received a grant of four hundred acres of land along the East Branch of the Conestoga in what is now Caernarvon Township. Jenkins lived in a cave for a while and eventually built a small stone house. In 1742, he sold his property to a Philadelphia merchant named William Branson. Branson built some iron forges on the property and a mansion that he named Windsor after the Windsor castle in England. Two years later, he deeded his estate to his four daughters. The youngest daughter, Elizabeth, married Lynford Lardner, who was one of William Penn's land commissioners and also happened to be Penn's brother-in-law. In 1750, Lardner moved to Windsor and took over management of the forges along with his wife's sisters. In 1758, David Jenkins, the son of John, became clerk at the Windsor forges. After Elizabeth Lardner's death, David Jenkins was able to purchase the shares from the Bransons' grandchildren and, by the time of the American Revolution, had ownership of his father's original four hundred acres plus hundreds more.[13]

David Jenkins's great-granddaughter Blanche Nevin lived in the mansion in 1899. She was a noted poet and sculptor. Her statue of Revolutionary

The Conestoga River

The mansion at Windsor Forge.

War general Peter Muhlenberg stands in the National Statuary Hall in Washington, D.C. She also sculpted the lion that still sits in Lancaster's Reservoir Park. Blanche's father, Dr. John Nevin, was a professor at Franklin and Marshall College and served as the school's president from 1866 to 1876. The mansion was listed in the National Register of Historic Places in 1990.

A short distance down the river from Windsor is Poole Forge. Poole Forge was built by James Old in 1779. James Old came to America from Wales and first worked as a puddler at Windsor Forge. Later, he built Speedwell Forge on the Hammer Creek, after which he purchased the Reading Furnace. The Reading Furnace produced large quantities of cannon and shot for Washington's army during the Revolutionary War. After the war, Old moved to Caernarvon Township, where he owned a gristmill on the Conestoga. It was on this property that he built his new forge. In 1785, Old sold the Speedwell Forge to his son-in-law, Robert Coleman, who will come into this story a bit later.

Another Welshman named Cyrus Jacobs also worked at Windsor for a while. Jacobs married one of James Old's daughters, after which he moved to Hammer Creek and managed his father-in-law's forges there. After James Old died, Jacobs took ownership of Poole Forge, where he became one of

A HISTORY

The Poole Forge mansion, built by James Old in 1779.

Lancaster County's most successful iron masters. Jacobs built another forge farther down the Conestoga at Spring Grove. The iron master's mansion at Spring Grove is still standing today, along with a gristmill that is no longer operating. The Spring Grove mansion was placed in the National Register of Historic Places in 1984.

ROCK FORD

Irishman Edward Hand came to Lancaster in 1775 to practice medicine. Hand had been a surgeon's mate with the Eighteenth Irish Regiment of Foot stationed at Fort Pitt. Soon after arriving at Lancaster, however, the "shot heard 'round the world" was fired at Lexington, marking the beginning of the American Revolutionary War. Hand joined the Continental army as lieutenant colonel of the First Battalion of Pennsylvania Rifleman in July 1775. He led troops in several campaigns and ended up as adjutant general to George Washington in 1781. After the war ended, he returned to Lancaster, where he bought a tract of land near the Conestoga River on which to build a farm. At that time, land under cultivation was called a "plantation," Hand

Edward Hand's 1794 Rock Ford mansion after a fresh snowfall.

called his plantation Rock Ford because it was near a ford across the river. There is an outcrop of rock along the river close by that later became known as Indian Rock. This may have figured in the name choice, or perhaps the ford had a rocky bottom.

Edward Hand and his wife Katherine "Kitty" moved in 1794 to Rock Ford, where they raised their eight children. Edward became active in politics and served in Congress and the Pennsylvania General Assembly and served as burgess of Lancaster. General and Mrs. Hand entertained George Washington for tea when the president visited Lancaster. This presumably took place at Rock Ford. In addition to the Hand family, the plantation was home to many other servants and laborers, both enslaved and free. The estate was sold after Edward and Katherine's deaths and operated as a tenant farm for some 150 years. In the 1950s, the mansion was slated for demolition to make way for a landfill and trash incinerator. The Junior League of Lancaster rescued the house and adjoining property in 1957. In May of the following year, the Rock Ford Foundation was formed to maintain the property. Today, the mansion has been restored and operates as museum.

A History

ROBERT FULTON AND THE STEAMBOAT

Robert Fulton was born on November 14, 1765, at a farm in Little Britain Township, Lancaster County. Fulton did not invent the steamboat, as some falsely claim, but he was the first to make steam-powered navigation commercially viable. The first steamboat on the Conestoga was built by the Lancastrian gunsmith William Henry in 1763. Henry had visited James Watt in England and brought back some steam engine knowledge. Henry designed a stern wheel–powered steamboat and tested it on the Conestoga River. Unfortunately, the engine produced such strong vibrations that it beat itself to pieces. Another American gunsmith and inventor, John Fitch, visited William Henry's shop, where Henry was pleased to share his designs for a steam engine with the inventor.

John Fitch designed a steam-powered boat and ran it on the Delaware River in August 1787. This boat carried passengers but was not financially profitable. In December 1787, James Rumsey demonstrated a steam-powered boat on the Potomac. Likewise, that boat did not prove to be commercially viable. Fitch and Rumsey both vied for the honor of being known as the inventor of the steamboat.

Robert Fulton also visited William Henry's gun shop as a teenager, and it is where the seed may have been planted for his later work.[14] Legend has it that when Robert was a boy in Lancaster County, he and a friend built a fishing skiff that was powered by hand-driven paddles and tested it on the Conestoga (hence the claim that Fulton conducted his first experiments with paddle wheels on the Conestoga). As a young man, he made a comfortable living painting portraits and landscapes and illustrating

This plaque, near Rock Ford, commemorates Robert Fulton's first experiments with paddleboats.

houses and machinery. In 1786, he traveled to Europe, where he continued painting for several years until he discovered that his true passion was mechanics and became a civil engineer. He invented a submarine that he called a "torpedo" in 1801 and tried to market the invention as a naval vessel first to the French and later to the English. Neither of them would commit to developing his invention, so he returned to New York in 1806. While in New York, he teamed up with Robert Livingston to develop the first commercially successful steamboat. His boat, the *Clermont*, carried passengers on the Hudson River. Later, Fulton moved to the Mississippi, where he demonstrated that a self-powered boat could move upstream against strong currents. Numerous businesses and institutions carry the Fulton name today. There is Fulton Township, Fulton Street, the Fulton Bank and, of course, the Fulton Theatre in downtown Lancaster.

LEMAN RIFLE-WORKS

In 1834, Henry Leman (1812–1887) built a forge and rifle barrel boring operation on the Conestoga near where the Lititz Run joins the river. This was located near the town of Catfish, now called Oregon. Today, the

A stone arch bridge spans the Lititz Run at Pinetown.

area is called Pinetown. Leman produced good-quality yet comparatively inexpensive flint-lock rifles with forty-two-inch barrels. The rifles were used for the western Indian trade initially, and later, he landed contracts with the U.S. government. Several hundred rifle barrels were manufactured at the mill on the Conestoga. In 1850, the mill was abandoned when Henry moved his factory to the city of Lancaster on the corner of Walnut and Cherry.[15] Remains of the mill were still standing in 1972 when they were finally destroyed by the flood caused by Hurricane Agnes.

BRINGING WATER TO LANCASTER CITY

For the first one hundred plus years after the founding of the town of Lancaster, its inhabitants had to rely on wells, pumps and springs for their water supply. As early as 1789, General Hand, who was serving as burgess at the time, lamented about the millions of gallons of water going to "waste" in the Conestoga River every year. But the prospect of bringing water from the river up to the town was considered an impossibility at that time.

Thirty-six years later, in 1829, the formation of the Lancaster Water Company was authorized by the state legislature, which also granted the company to sell stock. Not much happened until 1831 when the legislature granted the city the right to levy taxes to support the water works.[16] The city hired engineer W.B. Mitchell to survey the possible options, and finally in 1836, Lancaster's first water plant was built on the site of a former mill and dam. This was located southeast of the city at the lower end of City Mill Road. A water wheel powered a series of pumps that carried water from the river up to the newly built reservoir on King Street next to the county jail. On Washington's birthday, February 21, 1837, the construction was completed and water from the Conestoga began to flow through water plugs in the city. Nothing was said, and presumably, not much consideration was given to what happened to the additional wastewater that was produced by this system. The water returned through the various conduits back to the Roaring Brook and finally back into the Conestoga, including any materials that were added to the mix in the process.

The abundance of water inspired some of the more well-to-do citizens to install bathtubs in their homes. The first to do so was Jacob Demuth, who installed a tub in 1839. Soon after, there were found to be eight more tubs in city homes. At this, the city council assessed a bathtub tax of three

The Conestoga River

The Second Lancaster Water Works (1888) appears through the arches of the Conestoga Viaduct. *Courtesy of LancasterHistory, Lancaster, Pennsylvania.*

dollars annually. Nine out of ten doctors of that time were unconvinced that such frequent bathing was healthy. The tenth doctor, Dr. John Light Atlee, begged to differ and installed a tub in his home in 1849. Even though the cholera outbreaks of 1832 and 1854 were blamed on "misty clouds of putrefying organic matter decaying along the streams and canals," Dr. Atlee believed the disease might be caused by some tiny organisms he could see in his microscope. He was proven correct thirty years later when germ theory became better understood.[17]

In 1888, the old water plant at the city mill was replaced with a new pumping station along the Conestoga River near the railroad bridge on Grofftown Road. Two large steam pumps operated with a daily capacity of eleven million gallons. These were placed on a reserve basis in 1929, when eight electrically driven and three gasoline-powered pumps were installed. The current water-treatment plant located along the Susquehanna River in Columbia was constructed in the 1950s. The Grofftown Road plant was removed in 1976. A small reserve pumping station is located across the river next to Conestoga Pines Park.

A History

ICE

Ever since colonial times, the river was a source of ice for the city and surrounding area. In the winter, when the river was frozen, men would cut the ice into large blocks using iron saws made for the purpose. The ice blocks were stored in icehouses that lined the riverbank. These houses could be as much as three stories tall and were packed with ice from floor to ceiling. The ice blocks were covered in straw and sawdust to prevent melting. Throughout the year, but especially during the summer months, the ice man would make his way through the back alleys with his horse-drawn cart bringing ice to the people who had iceboxes in their homes. Sometimes the boxes were built into the wall with an outside opening so the ice man could refill the box without needing to enter the home. In other cases, the delivery man had to enter the kitchen with a block of ice in his tongs to be placed into the family's icebox. When manufactured ice became available in 1895, the need to harvest ice from the river declined. Household refrigeration started to become available in 1925. Today, we simply need to push a button on the front of our refrigerator door to fill our cup with crushed ice.

Chapter 3

SLACK-WATER NAVIGATION

Lancaster became the capital of Pennsylvania in 1799, but the capital moved to Harrisburg in 1812. By the turn of the century, Baltimore had become a ready market for agricultural goods and could be reached by natural and modified waterways, thereby reducing the traffic from Lancaster to Philadelphia.[18] Lancaster's leaders, called burgesses at that time, were in search of ways to improve the local economy. In 1817, the State of New York began a major project to connect its eastern ports with Lake Erie in the west. That caused a stir in Pennsylvania, which then began a major push to build canals across the state, fueled by fears that New York would threaten commerce in Philadelphia. On March 27, 1824, Governor Andrew Shulze appointed the first three Pennsylvania canal commissioners and charged them with the task of finding a viable canal route connecting Lancaster and Chester Counties to Pittsburgh. The construction of the Pennsylvania Canal officially commenced with an act of the Pennsylvania legislature on February 25, 1826. The "canal fever" ran high among Pennsylvania business leaders during this time. The Pennsylvania Canal Commission determined that it would not be feasible to dig a canal between Philadelphia and Columbia and opted instead to traverse that section with a railroad. This railroad portion of the Main Line of Public Works came right through Lancaster City.

A History

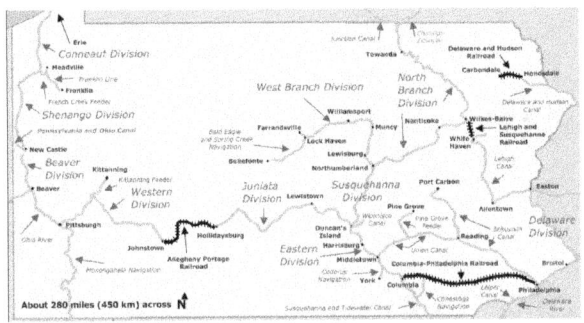

Map of Pennsylvania Canals.
Public domain.

THE CONESTOGO NAVIGATION COMPANY

On May 15, 1824, at a public meeting in Lancaster, a committee was formed to petition the state legislature to grant rights to incorporate a company to make the waters of the Conestogo navigable. The petition was granted on March 3, 1825. This act provided for the "erection of the Conestogo Navigation Company and the construction of its plant." Adam Reigart and others should have the power to make a navigation canal or slack-water navigation and towpath on and along the Conestogo River and to set up locks and dams fit for navigation. Landowners should be compensated for any damages caused by erecting the dams or by the swelling water. The act provided a penalty for not keeping the dams in repair. The company would be able to sell or rent surplus water for works.[19] The capital stock of the company was fixed as 1,200 shares of stock at $50 per share ($60,000).

This was not the first attempt to make the Conestogo navigable. On March 17, 1805, the Pennsylvania Assembly passed an act authorizing a lawyer by the name of William Webb to improve the navigation on the Conestoga River using locks and dams. Webb's idea was to make the river navigable from its mouth on the Susquehanna to Witmer's bridge, located on the east side of the borough of Lancaster where the Philadelphia turnpike crossed the river. Nothing was done under his charter, and it expired.[20] Fifteen years later, on March 28, 1820, another prominent lawyer in Lancaster, James Hopkins, obtained a charter to form the Conestoga Slack-Water Navigation Company to make the river navigable. Hopkins had previously made an unsuccessful attempt to build a canal around the Conewago Falls on the east side of the Susquehanna River. Unfortunately, that canal was poorly laid out and not useful for navigation. This charter for Conestogo navigation specified that the locks should be eighteen feet wide and eighty feet long. It also stipulated that a horn should announce the approach of boats at least a

The title from Ephraim Beach's proposal for Conestogo Navigation.

quarter mile away from the locks.[21] Mr. Hopkins did not act on his charter, and his rights also expired.

By June 1825, enough shares had been secured that the governor issued a charter to the Conestoga Navigation Company. The company was organized in July at a meeting held at the house of innkeeper John Steman. The managers were Adam Reigart, Edward Coleman, George B. Porter, Jasper Slaymaker, John F. Steinman, George Louis Meyer and Hugh Maxwell (all of Lancaster City) and John Litner and George Haverstick of Lancaster Township. The committee engaged the services of an engineer named Captain Ephraim Beach to survey the Conestoga and draw up plans to make the waterway navigable. Captain Beach produced a map in November of that year that laid out a series of locks and canals from Reigart's Landing on the southern end of the city to the Susquehanna River. Captain Beach introduced short canals to reduce the number of locks that would be required. This, he said, would reduce the cost of maintaining the locks and their dams. The board, on the other hand, was adamant that the system should consist entirely of slack-water navigation with no canals.

A History

SLACK-WATER NAVIGATION

What is slack-water navigation? In the minutes of the board of managers, they described it as "a connected system of ponds formed by dams and locks entirely independent of canals."[22] A typical canal was constructed as a separate channel dug along the banks of another watercourse. This canal was flanked by a towpath and would have locks at regular intervals to account for the change in elevation.

In a slack-water system, dams were constructed at intervals across the width of the river. This resulted in the water piling up behind the dams to form "ponds." The dams were spaced such that the water behind one dam would back up all the way to the next dam upstream. This usually amounted to several miles of navigable water wide enough for animal-powered packet boats to be pulled along the side while steam-powered craft could navigate the center of the channel. Locks were constructed as an integral part of each dam. On the Conestoga, the towpath and all the locks were built on the left side of the river while traveling downstream.

Advantages of slack-water navigation compared to a canal:

- Suitable for all sorts of craft. "It is a beautiful river for steamboats. Whenever the Susquehanna is made navigable, we shall sail in them to the cities on our seaboard."[23]
- Speed. "The greater expanse of water permits crafts of larger burden to be employed than on canals; and it has been demonstrated that vessels of the same dimensions are drawn with less expense of power and with more celerity than on canals. This has been satisfactorily tested on that part of the work which has been completed, the common rate of a packet boat, 60 feet by keel and 12 feet beam, with 100 passengers on board, drawn by two horses, being found to average six miles per hour. The same power applied to a similar packet, upon a canal of the width, experience justifies us in saying will not exceed three miles per hour, consequently the number of boats, horses, and hands, employed to convey the same tonnage, for a given number of miles upon the Conestoga, is, to the number employed upon a canal, as three is to six, which, of course, produces a relative difference in the cost of transportation."[24]
- Fewer locks per mile. The ponds provided a minimum of four feet of draft at their upper ends but could be considerably

deeper above the dams. This allowed for a longer expanse of water with more vertical drop between the locks. Fewer locks per mile translated into faster overall traversal times.
- Cost to build. A traditional canal required a ditch to be dug along the entire route. Slack-water navigation just required a series of dams and locks to be constructed on the existing stream.
- Waterpower. "At eight of the dams we have on each side of the basin sites for water works with seven to nine feet fall, with a prism of water unrivalled."[25]
- Recreation in the ponds. The dams slowed the flow of the water and produced beautiful areas for recreational boating and fishing, as well as ice skating in the winter.

These are the advantages. There were disadvantages as well, but they were not very noticeable to the engineers of the nineteenth century. The ecological impact of the sediment collected behind the dams would not be understood until more than a century later.

CONSTRUCTION BEGINS

On August 22, 1825, the company sent out a request for bids. The proposal was for twelve dams and locks with an average lift of five feet. In September, Adam Reigart, John Reynolds and Jasper Slaymaker accompanied the engineers Captain Ephraim Beach and Simeon Guilford to survey the river and determine the locations of the locks. The entire distance by the course of the stream was seventeen miles, seventy-one chains (a chain equals sixty-six feet). The whole fall was about sixty-four feet and at this time was divided into nine ponds. The ponds had an average width of two hundred feet and were "never less than four feet deep in the channel."[26]

In December, the board awarded the construction contract to Mr. Caleb Hammill from New York State. Hammill was to complete the work by July 4, 1827, at a cost of $53,240. Ephraim Beach was asked to superintend the works of the company but declined, citing ill health. Guilford also declined for unknown reasons. Hammill then selected Edward F. Gay, a pupil of Canvass White, who was chief engineer of the Union Canal, as the engineer to oversee the project. After completing this project, Edward Gay went on to become the chief engineer of the Pennsylvania Canal, the Columbia and Philadelphia Railroad and the Susquehanna and Tidewater Canal.

A History

On July 31, 1826, the first dam and lock were completed at Martin Light's mill. Two days later, the board of managers, on the invitation of Hammill, going aboard the new boat *Edward Coleman*, proceeded at the rate of five miles an hour to the new lock. There was a band of music on the boat playing national airs. Upon reaching the lock, they found a committee of ladies from Lancaster, with Judge Moulton C. Rogers and Dr. Samuel Humes. After the boat entered the lock, Mrs. William Jenkins made an address on behalf of the ladies, complimenting Hammill on his success in the work so far and stating the great advantages it would give to the people of the county. She ended by presenting the contractor with a flag. Hammill responded in an appropriate speech, and the ladies and their escorts were taken aboard the boat, which proceeded to Reigart's Landing, at the head of navigation, a distance of two and three-quarter miles. Later in the afternoon, the boat returned to the bridge, where the party disembarked and returned to Lancaster.[27]

As the construction progressed, the company needed more funds. The company had purchased Light's mill (lock #1) in 1826, Haverstick's mill (lock #2) in 1827 and Espenshade's mill on the Little Conestoga (lock #6) in 1828. The managers made a plea to call in the pledges of stockholders who had not yet paid their installments. They also tried unsuccessfully to borrow $20,000 from local banks using the mill property at lock #1 as collateral. Finally, in October 1827, a loan of $5,000 was granted by the Farmers Bank of Lancaster if the company mortgaged its estate. Engineer Gay was projecting a completion date of November 1827; however, as a harbinger of what was to come, an especially severe flood occurred on the Conestoga in October that destroyed some of the dams and damaged others, causing the completion date to be postponed. In December, the board petitioned the state legislature for authorization to mortgage the property, tolls and other profits as security for a loan. The petition was granted on December 20.

Finally, on January 2, 1829, Engineer Gay reported to the president and board of managers the entire completion of the work from the landing of Adam Reigart to where the Conestoga empties into the Susquehanna.[28] It was a distance of seventeen miles and seventy-one chains, with a fall of sixty-four feet, making valuable water power at each of the locks. Early in the progress, it was found necessary to increase the strength of the locks in order to resist the great pressure of the water. This extra work cost $6,573, bringing the total cost to $59,534. Other bills were added later, bringing the total cost of making the Conestoga navigable to $68,539.92.

The Conestoga River

OPERATIONS BEGIN

The company opened for business in the spring of 1829. An entry in *Hazard's Register* on March 17, 1829, reports:

> *Captain Charles Odel took on board 90 hogsheads of whisky and left lock #4 at 5pm and arrived at Port Deposit by 2am. The charges for delivering to Baltimore was one cent per gallon. On the 19th, Captain Omit loaded two arks*[29] *with whisky and flour at lock #8 for shipping to Baltimore. Two other arks are loaded with whisky of ninety hogshead and will proceed this day. The navigation is in fine order, and the people expect to be benefited with an active Spring trade and that from the port of Lancaster we can always get to Baltimore two or three weeks earlier than trade of the west branch of the Susquehanna, owing to the late improvements in navigation.*[30]

Ellis and Evans's *History of Lancaster County* reports:

> *In one day in May, 1829, there arrived at Lancaster one ark-load of coal for George L. Meyer and P.W. Reigart; one raft of boards for the same parties; one ark-load of coal for William Russell; one ark-load of wood for the same; two rafts of boards and logs for railroad; two arks, with one hundred and sixty thousand shingles and ten thousand feet of boards, brought by Mr. Reeves from the State of New York; one raft of boards for the same; one ark of boards and shingles for Levi Rogers; two rafts of boards, and lumber for same; one ark-load of locust posts for Dr. A. Carpenter; one ark-load of boards for Israel Cooper. The fact that these were but the arrivals of a single day indicates the great amount of business done on the navigation.*[31]

In addition to the *Edward Coleman* mentioned previously, there were several other boats built at this time for navigating on the Conestoga. Captain John Mitchell built a packet boat[32] seventy feet long with a twelve-foot beam that had three cabins: one for ladies, one for gentlemen and one for the dining room. Samuel Slaymaker, one of the proprietors of the stage line between Lancaster and Philadelphia, built a pleasure boat that was sixty feet long and twelve feet wide, which was drawn by two horses and was used on the first pond between Reigart's Landing and the first lock.[33] A packet boat named the *Red Rover* was built in Lancaster in 1828 and ran between Lancaster and Safe Harbor until 1833.

Unfortunately, later in the same month a flood damaged lock #9 at the Susquehanna. An entry in *Hazard's Register* dated May 12, 1829, states that "yesterday morning as the ark of Adam Reigart was clearing lock No. 9, at the mouth of the Conestoga, part of the wall fell on the ark and hurled it into the river, a complete wreck." Operations were ceased for the rest of that year while repairs were made to the damaged lock. The City of Lancaster advanced $10,000 for two hundred shares of stock to fund the repairs.[34]

Business began again in the spring of 1830. The tolls collected in 1829 were $310.45. In 1830, the tolls were $1,430, and in 1831, the revenue was $2,243. The company seemed to be on its way to profitability. An entry in *Hazard's Register* in 1832 stated, "Lumber and coal business has increased for the last two years to an amazing extent and it must increase every succeeding year. Coal received by the Conestoga Navigation Company sold at Lancaster from $.50 to $.75 a ton cheaper than at Columbia or Marietta, charging land carriage to Lancaster; and boards and shingles from $.50 to $.75 per one thousand feet less."

DISASTER STRIKES

Then, in January 1832, a large ice flood on the Conestoga destroyed many of the dams. A committee of stockholders was formed to examine the extent of the damages and assess the probable expense of making repairs. After reviewing the damages, the committee made the following report:

> *Lock No. 1 is injured. The outside crib or wall is razed to its foundation. The land crib is injured but not near so much as the other. The gallows frames are removed and some of them are gone. All the gates are there but they are removed from their position, and therefore injured. This dam is permanent.*
>
> *No. 2. The walls of this lock are but little injured. The planking is there; the gates are shattered but not lost; the gallows frames are all removed. The dam is slightly affected.*
>
> *No. 3. A beautiful lock and dam, is safe, awaiting the commerce of the river.*
>
> *No. 4. Where our toll house stands is not marked by the ice flood.*
>
> *No. 5 is solid and sound.*
>
> *No. 6 reposes in safety.*

No. 7. The gates of this lock are injured, but they can easily be repaired. Some of the gallows frames are removed.

No. 8. More injured than lock 7, the lock walls are standing, but the gates and nearly all the gallows frames are removed and injured, and the dam in part torn away.

No. 9. The unfortunate!! The crib walls of this lock are standing after bearing all the fury of the ice of the Susquehanna last winter. The gallows frames are all gone. The planking of the cribs is in part removed and some of the stones displaced. The gates are removed, and though all found, they are much injured. The dam is razed to its foundation, but that stands unmoved.

The Towpath needed repairs with the greater part being bridge over the Mill Creek.[35]

SHERIFF SALE

After assessing the damage and estimating the cost to repair them, the committee recommended that the repairs should be made to "leave it as a rich legacy to our city and to our posterity." The committee also recommended that the company offer the water power at the dams for rent as a way of increasing its revenue. Unfortunately, the company was unable to raise the funds necessary to make the needed repairs and was subsequently sold at a sheriff's sale on June 1, 1833. Sheriff Adam Bear sold to William and Edward Coleman the whole property of the Conestoga Navigation Company, which included a stone gristmill in Conestoga Township along with "all the dams, locks, sluices, roads, paths, towpaths, water and water works thereunto belonging and all the houses, mills, lands, tenements and hereditaments and real estate of and belonging to the said Conestoga Navigation Company lying on both sides of Conestoga river in Lampeter, Conestoga, Lancaster and Manor townships; and all the tolls, incomes, rents, issues, profits, rights, liberties, privileges, franchises, hereditaments whatsoever belonging thereto." The price for the estate was $17,500.

A History

THE LANCASTER, SUSQUEHANNA AND SLACKWATER NAVIGATION COMPANY

Soon after the sheriff's sale in June 1833, William Coleman sold his half-interest in the company to his brother, Edward. Edward Coleman now owned all the lands and rights of the defunct Conestoga Navigation Company. Coleman repaired the dams and bought tracts of land for towpaths and flowage rights at a cost of $120,000. The dam at Slackwater was raised to a height of twenty feet and three inches. Coleman then chartered a new company called the Lancaster, Susquehanna and Slackwater Navigation Company. The company was chartered on April 1, 1837. The corporation consisted of Edward Coleman, George Louis Mayer, Peter Long, Abram Peters and Jacob Huber. After the company was formed, Coleman sold all his holdings to the new company for the price of $200,000 on May 6, 1840.[36] According to the deed, the system at that time consisted of nine locks and dams; however, Coleman eventually eliminated the two locks below Rock Hill, bringing the total count to seven. The year 1840 also marked the completion of the Susquehanna and Tidewater Canal along the west side of the Susquehanna. An entry lock to the canal was placed across from the mouth of the Conestoga. A crib dam across the Susquehanna provided enough draft for the canalboats to be towed across the river by steam tugs.[37]

In 1838, the secretary of war recommended in his annual report that a national foundry be established for the manufacture of cannon for use in the army and navy of the United States. A committee was formed to recommend Lancaster as the preferred site of the National Foundry. The committee consisted of David Longenecker, S. Dale, J.K. Findlay, C. Hager, Thomas E. Franklin and George B. Kerfoot. The committee was chaired by the Honorable William Cost Johnson. On January 12, 1839, the committee released a report in which it cited the Lancaster, Susquehanna and Slackwater Navigation Company as one of the many assets of Lancaster.

> *There are on the Conestoga river, between the city of Lancaster and its mouth, (a distance, by the course of the stream, of sixteen miles), nine dams, having a fall of from six to fourteen feet each, making an aggregate fall of sixty-four feet. These dams have all been constructed by the Conestogo Navigation Company, for the purpose of the navigation, and afford at each dam an immense surplus of waterpower, capable of easy application to the contemplated establishment. The river has an average width of about two hundred and twenty feet, and discharges upwards of twelve millions of cubic feet of water per diem.*[38]

The Conestoga River

In November 1843, the city councils were invited to an "experimental excursion" on the Conestoga. The invitation was sent from the Lancaster, Susquehanna and Slackwater Navigation Company and delivered to the councils by Mayor John Mathiot. The councils promptly accepted with the following reply:

> *That Councils feel great pleasure in hearing of the arrival of the Steamboat, "The Edward Coleman," which is to be run on the Conestoga from the city to tidewater, and hail the occurrence as indicative of the completion of what they had always believed would be of great benefit to the city and county of Lancaster.*
>
> *Councils feel deeply the compliment paid to them, and freely accept, by resolving to meet at their rooms on Tuesday morning at 8 o'clock, to proceed from there to Mr. Reigart's Landing.*

What follows is an extract from a newspaper article written shortly after.

> *Before the Edward Coleman had gotten up steam, a roll-call registered the nine Select and the fifteen Common members all aboard on schedule time. As the weather was a little too cool for bathing outwardly in the placid waters of the Susquehanna, our caravan of sightseers were not to be blamed for bathing themselves inwardly from a dozen bottles of champagne at the Company's expense! Then to think of the ample "spread," so different from what they had been getting at home! What actually occurred in passing through the locks would be to betray confidence. It was late in the day when Safe Harbor was reached, owing to "The Edward Coleman" running out of steam. On our homeward journey, trouble beset us on every hand, requiring the packet boat to be drawn homeward bound by three mules. And now, Mr. Editor, whether any prayers were offered by the returning councilmen is extremely doubtful owing to the fact that they were not prayerfully inclined.*[39]

OPEN FOR BUSINESS

The navigation company operated fairly successfully for the next fifteen to twenty years. On May 28, 1844, an ad ran in Lancaster's newspaper *The Intelligencer* that stated:

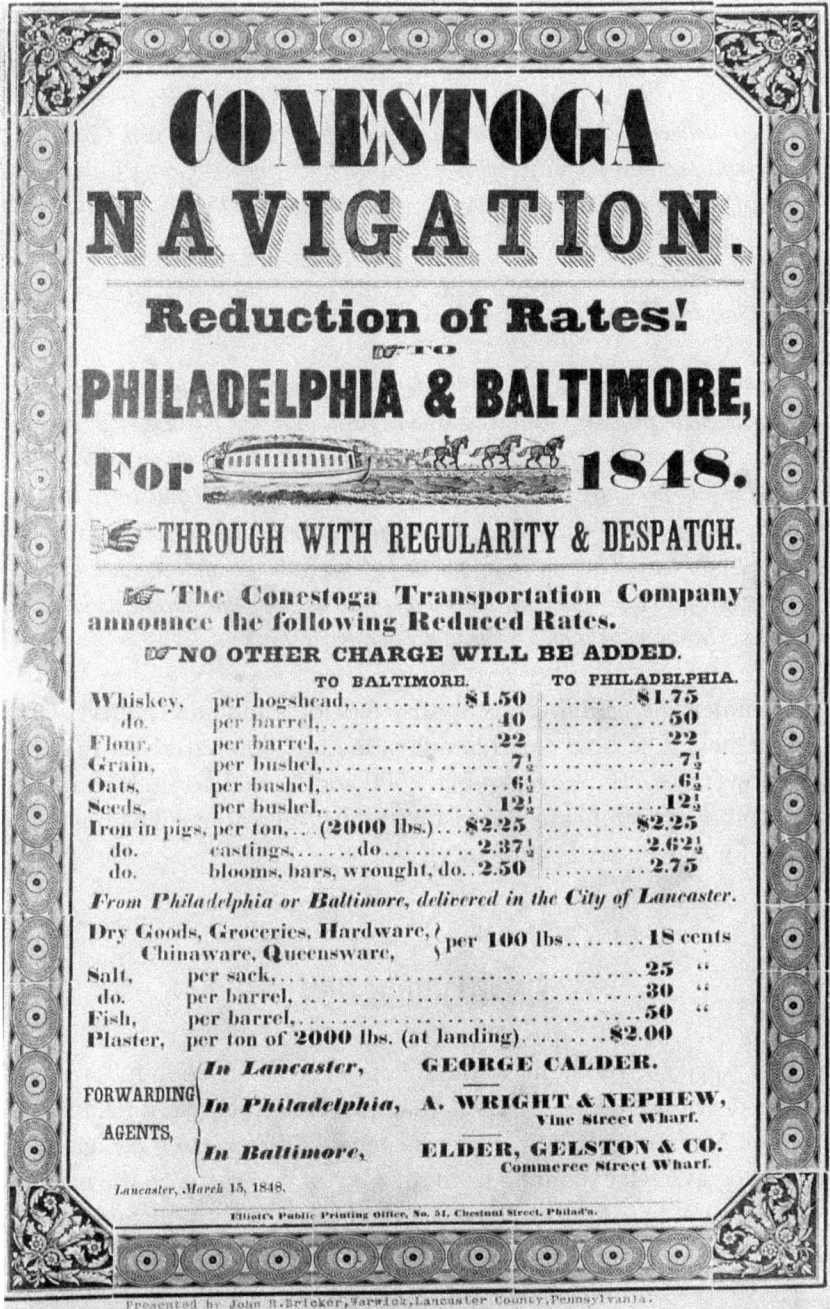

Conestoga Navigation rate table, 1848. *Courtesy of LancasterHistory, Lancaster, Pennsylvania.*

> *The splendid new Iron Steamboat CONESTOGA is now running with regularity and great dispatch between Lancaster & Philadelphia, and will take freight either way at very reduced rates, viz.: Flour at 18½ cents per barrel, delivered in Broad Street or any part of Philadelphia. Store Goods 16 cents per 100 lbs. delivered in Lancaster city. Apply to George Calder, Graeff's Landing, Lancaster. A Wright & Nephew, Vine St., Wharf, Philadelphia.*

In the *Philadelphia Gazette*, the following appeared:

> *We mentioned a few days since, the departure from this city for Lancaster, on the new steamer* Conestoga. *She performed the passage, via the Chesapeake and Delaware Canal, to the entire satisfaction of the proprietors, discharging her cargo, and has now returned with another full cargo of iron, having also in tow a barge loaded with iron, the two cargoes making about 100 tons. This settles the question of navigation in that channel; the* Conestoga *will resume her trips tomorrow, as a regular packet, at low rates. Messrs. Wright and Nephew are agents for this boat.*

The steamer *Conestoga* was seventy-five feet long and had cabins for ladies and gentlemen. The hold could handle a load of 600 barrels of flour, with enough power to tow barges carrying 1,500 additional barrels. It could make the trip from Philadelphia to Lancaster in thirty-two hours. The boat was in operation for sixteen years until 1856.

FINAL LIQUIDATION

Finally, on April 16, 1866, the whole system once again went up for sheriff's sale. The deed at that time stated that the Lancaster, Susquehanna and Slackwater Navigation Company consisted of "Slackwater navigation on the Conestoga Creek extending from the City of Lancaster to the mouth of the Conestoga at Safe Harbor, 17 miles, connecting it with the Susquehanna Canal, with seven locks and dams and one grand lock, and six lock houses."[40] The system was sold to Samuel J. Reeves, owner of the Safe Harbor Iron Works, for $10,000.

A History

THE NINE LOCKS

The locks had heavy wooden gates at each end mounted on hinges that allowed them to swivel open into the lock. There were indentations in the lock walls such that the gates were flush with the wall when opened. The gates had "wickets" at the bottom that were opened or closed with metal handles on the top of the gate. The locks worked like a kind of water-powered elevator. When the elevator was in the "up" position, the downstream gates were closed, and the lock was filled with water to the level of the upper pond. The upper gates were opened, and a barge could enter the lock from the upstream side. Once the boat was tied off in the lock, the upper gates were closed. Next, the wickets on the lower gate were turned open. This allowed the water to gradually drain out of the lock, lowering the boat in the process. When the water was fully drained, the lower gates were opened and the boat could exit the lock and continue downstream. Now the "elevator" was in the down position ready to receive a boat traveling upstream. The procedure was reversed to fill the lock with water and raise the boat to the upper level.

The original system included nine locks. Nine are listed in the report to the stockholders in 1832. The report of the committee to recommend Lancaster as the site of a national foundry in 1839 also lists nine locks being parcel to the Lancaster, Susquehanna and Slackwater Navigation Company. An article in the January 22, 1840 edition of the *Lancaster Examiner* states that when Edward Coleman rebuilt the locks and dams, he eliminated two of the locks, bringing the count to seven. At the time of the final sale in 1866, the deed listed seven locks and dams. The map that appears as an insert in Earl Rebman's book *Conestoga Watershed: Outline of History* shows only six locks, but that map does not include the exit lock at Safe Harbor, which is clearly visible on an 1852 map of Manor Township. Like Rebman's map, the Manor Township map does not show the original locks 6 and 7 between Rock Hill and Safe Harbor. For our purposes here, I will always number the locks as it was when there were nine.

It should be noted that there is some disagreement about the locations of some of these locks. I am using the locations published by the American Canal Society.[41] Some sources claim there was a lock between Wabank and Slackwater, making the lock at Slackwater number 5. I do not believe this to be the case because the 1832 report to the shareholders clearly states that the tollhouse was at lock number 4. The tollhouse and maintenance shop were located on the canal at Slackwater. The Lancaster County bridge archives also labels the covered bridge at Slackwater as the "Lock 4 bridge."

The head of navigation was located at Reigart's Landing on the south side of Lancaster City. Adam Reigart (president of the first Navigation Company) operated an inn near where the stagecoach road from Philadelphia crossed a bridge over the Conestoga. This was approximately where the entrance to the Lancaster County Park is today. The inn was demolished in the 1950s.[42] Today, there is a small neighborhood nearby that bears the name Reigart's Landing.

The second principal landing point was a place called Graeff's (or Graff's) Landing at the foot of Prince and Queen Streets. George Graeff built a two-story tavern there in the late 1700s. At the time when the Conestoga Navigation was operating, the tavern was known as the Engleside Hotel. The "landing" would have been on the south side of the river due to the location of the towpath on that side. Today, the Engleside Hotel is called the Distelfink Inn.

TABLE 2: LOCKS

Lock	Lift	Width	Coordinates	Notes
1	7	265	40.010554, -76.302896	Remains of Levan's Mill dam and headrace still visible
2	6	300	40.003469, -76.313651	Lock mostly intact
3	8	355	39.997843, -76.328486	Remains of dam and wall still visible
4	9	225	39.981667, -76.357605	No remains of dam; remains of canal visible
5	6	280	39.962707, -76.364556	Remains of power plant visible
6	9	285	39.949887, -76.367792*	Estimated location
7	7	210	39.946829, -76.378718*	Estimated location
8/6	6	220	39.939585, -76.386913	Lock mostly intact behind fence
9/7	8	180	39.928893, -76.383746	No discernable remains

A History

LOCK #1, LIGHT'S MILL

Lock #1 was located at Martin Light's Mill along the road from Lancaster to Martic Forge, now the New Danville Pike (Route 324). A historical marker marks this location. This was two and three-quarters of a mile below the head of navigation at Reigart's Landing. The Conestoga Navigation Company purchased this mill on April 4, 1826, for $5,500. The first lock was completed on July 31, 1826.

LOCK #2, HAVERSTICK'S MILL

The Conestoga Navigation Company purchased Haverstick's Mill on June 7, 1827, along with fifty-seven acres of land. The remains of the second lock can still be seen on private property near the old bridge abutments from the Second Lock Covered Bridge.

LOCK #3, WABANK (HEINEY'S MILL)

Lock #3 was located just downstream of where Millersville Road (Route 741) crosses the river today. There had been an earlier covered bridge just below the lock at the end of Short Lane. The remains of the dam are still visible on the riverbank. The dam was a timber-crib structure founded on rock, 280 feet long and 15 feet high. Water backed up 3.4 miles to the second lock mill site.

LOCK #4, SLACKWATER (ROHRER'S MILL)

The fourth lock was located at a place known as Petersburg, now called Slackwater. There was a tavern at this location as early as 1807. Despite the board's apparent dislike of canals, they dug a short canal at this location, most likely to accommodate their tollhouse. This was also the location of the company carpenter and maintenance crew. The dam at this lock was located just upstream from the old Slackwater covered bridge. The canal began at the dam and continued for about a quarter mile until it reentered the river.

The Conestoga River

Remains of Levan's Mill dam at the site of lock #1.

Remains of lock #2.

A History

Lock #3 at Wabank. *From* Canals Along the Lower Susquehanna, *by Gerald Smeltzer.*

Remains of the Wabank power plant at the site of lock #3.

LOCK #5, ROCK HILL

Lock #5 was located just above the Rock Hill iron bridge at the end of Long Lane. Remains of this lock and the power plant that replaced it can still be seen.

LOCK #6, ESPENSHADE'S MILL (KENDIG'S MILL)

Lock #6 was located about a half mile below where the Little Conestoga joins the big Conestoga. No remains are visible today. This lock was one of the original nine but was eliminated when Edward Coleman rebuilt the system. An 1852 map of Conestoga Township does not show this lock or dam.

LOCK #7

Lock #7 was located about a mile below lock #6 where the river makes a bend and Conestoga Boulevard cuts the corner. No remains can be seen today. Lock #7 had a seven-foot lift. This lock was also apparently eliminated by Edward Coleman.

LOCK #8, SAFE HARBOR

Lock #8 (later #6) was located at the north end of the village of Safe Harbor where River Road crosses the river. The dam for lock #8 supplied water for the Safe Harbor Iron Company even after navigation ceased. The remains of lock #8 can be seen behind a fence in the Safe Harbor park.

A History

Lock #4 and tollhouse on the canal at Slackwater. *Courtesy of LancasterHistory, Lancaster, Pennsylvania.*

Slackwater Canal today.

Remains of the power plant at Rock Hill, site of lock #5.

Remains of lock #8 at Safe Harbor Park.

The West Branch (*right*) joins the East Branch (*lower left*) to form the beginning of the Conestoga River in Caernarvon Township.

The upper Conestoga in summer on Limekiln Road.

Sunrise on the upper Conestoga along South Red School Road.

The river meanders the Conestoga Valley on the Fourth of July.

A pastoral scene along Boot Jack Road.

People enjoy a peaceful Sunday afternoon under the covered bridge at Poole Forge.

The Mill Road crosses the Conestoga on this light bridge.

The view looking downstream from the Mill Road bridge.

The river flows over an old mill dam under the Linden Road bridge. The sluice gate is in the foreground.

The pond behind the mill dam offers a prime fishing spot.

The gentle Conestoga flows through pastureland along Conestoga Road.

A mule enjoys some sweet grass by the river near Gristmill Road.

The pond above the dam at Kurtz's mill. The mill is no longer standing. The covered bridge that had been at this location is now in Lancaster Central Park.

A footbridge crosses the river along Cabin Drive. Railings optional.

The Brownstown Mill.

Bushong's Mill.

Pinetown Covered Bridge.

The view from a window on the Pinetown Bridge.

Swallows catch insects above the river along Mondale Road.

Kayakers paddle under the Hunsicker Mill Covered Bridge.

More paddlers float by Perelman Park.

An Amtrak train passes over the Conestoga River Viaduct.

The view looking upstream from the bridge at Bridgeport.

The sites of Rocky Springs and People's Bathing Resorts as they appear today.

The Carousel house at Rocky Springs.

Canada geese spend the night on the river near the Conestoga Greenway Trail.

An old sycamore leans over the river along the Conestoga Greenway Trail.

The Edward Hand mansion at Rock Ford after a fresh snowfall.

The tranquil Conestoga at Lancaster County Central Park.

Wildflowers adorn the trail at Windolph Landing Natural Area.

A blue heron watches for fish at Safe Harbor Park.

An autumn scene at Safe Harbor Park.

A History

LOCK #9

Lock 9 (later #7) was near to the mouth of the Conestoga at Safe Harbor (the "Port of Lancaster"), just south of the Safe Harbor Ironworks. Edward Coleman operated a sawmill here in 1839. This mill produced one million board-feet per year.[43] This lock and dam are visible on the 1852 map of Manor Township near where a small creek enters the Conestoga. This lock was obliterated by the construction of the Safe Harbor dam.

Above: Approximate location of lock #9 at Safe Harbor.

Left: Historical marker describing the "Port of Lancaster."

ADAM REIGART

Adam Reigart Jr. (1765–1844) was a prominent Lancaster citizen who seems to have been involved in many organizations around the borough/city. He apparently was well respected by his peers because he seems to have been elected president of every new enterprise in the town. His father, Adam Reigart Sr. (1739–1813), was an active participant in the American Revolution. He became lieutenant colonel of the First Battalion of the Lancaster County Militia and served under the command of George Ross. The elder Reigart was the proprietor of the Grape Hotel in Lancaster, which was an important meeting place for various committees on business related to American independence.

Adam Reigart Jr. was one of the managers of the Lancaster and Susquehanna Turnpike Company that incorporated on April 22, 1794. The company oversaw the construction of the highway between Lancaster and Columbia. He was also a manager of the Gap and Newport Turnpike Company, which formed in 1796, as well as the Lancaster and Middletown Turnpike, which formed in 1804. The Columbia Pike opened in 1807.

In the early 1800s, the burgesses of Lancaster decided they ought to have their own bank located in the town, and so the Lancaster Branch of the Pennsylvania Bank was formed. The bank opened on May 18, 1803, and Reigart was elected president. The bank was located at the northeast corner of King and Prince Streets.[44] A few years later, in 1807, the Lancaster and Susquehanna Insurance Company formed, and Reigart became that company's first president.

In 1813, the Union Fire Company of Lancaster underwent a reorganization. The fire company, which was formed in the 1760s, was only informally organized up until this time. The number of members was increased to fifty (from forty), and the first election of regular officers was held. Adam Reigart was elected president and served in that capacity until his death in 1844.[45]

From the incorporation of Lancaster as a borough in 1742 until it became a city, the town was governed by two burgesses and six assistants. Adam Reigart Jr. served as chief burgess of Lancaster borough from 1810 until 1815. When Lancaster became organized as a city in 1818, the city was governed by a mayor and select and common councils. Reigart was a member of the common council. In 1814, Reigart purchased the former residence of the tanner Michael Musser at 323 West King Street. Reigart added an addition and completely renovated the house. It is still standing today.

A History

When the Conestoga Navigation Company formed in 1825, Adam Reigart was elected president. He remained president until the company was sold to Edward Coleman in 1833. Reigart operated a hotel at the head of navigation called Reigart's Landing. Adam Reigart Jr. died on May 2, 1844, at the age of seventy-eight.

EDWARD COLEMAN

Who was Edward Coleman, and where did he get the money to make this investment? Edward Coleman was born on July 4, 1792, to Robert and Anne Caroline (Old) Coleman. Robert Coleman was the owner of Speedwell Forge, as well as two other forges on the Hammer Creek that were called the Upper and Lower Hopewell Forges. These should not be confused with the Hopewell Furnace that is on the French Creek. Robert was elected a member of the Pennsylvania Assembly in 1783 and served as an associate judge of Lancaster County for twenty years.[46] Robert died in 1825, and his sons—Edward, William, James and Thomas Bird—inherited his estate. Edward had two sisters, Anne Caroline and Sarah. Anne Caroline dated and became engaged to a Lancaster lawyer named James Buchanan. Her father disapproved of the engagement. Due to a misunderstanding, Anne broke off the engagement and retreated to Philadelphia, where she died suddenly, probably of an overdose of laudanum.[47] At this, James Buchanan vowed he would never marry and went on to be the only bachelor president of the United States. Edward's other sister, Sarah, was in love with the co-rector of St. James Episcopal Church in Lancaster. Her father disapproved of this relationship also. After her father's death in 1825, Sarah thought she would now be able to marry her lover. However, her father had granted his sons Edward and James the right to approve their sister's spouse. Edward had a disagreement with the rector and did not approve the marriage. Sarah then went off to Philadelphia, where she committed suicide.[48] Robert, William, Anne and Sarah are all buried in the cemetery at St. James in Lancaster.

Edward Coleman married Mary Jane Ross in 1816. He served in the state House of Representatives in 1818–19 and in the state Senate in 1820–24. In 1828, he built the Colemanville Forge on the site of the former Martic Forge along the Pequea Creek. Coleman owned a sawmill located at lock #9 in Safe Harbor. He was also one of the managers of the Susquehanna and Tidewater Canal that was incorporated in 1835.[49] Edward died on June 6, 1841, not long after the Lancaster, Susquehanna and Slackwater Navigation Company was founded.

Chapter 4

BRIDGES AND MILLS

*B*ridges were rare in the colonial period. Most rivers were crossed either by fording the stream or, if the river was too deep for fording, by ferry. For the smaller streams and wetlands, it was common to lay a row of logs in the stream parallel to the water flow. The horses and wagons would cross over the logs to avoid getting mired in the mud. The bumpy ride over the logs gave rise to the term "corduroy roads." As time progressed and the population increased, more bridges were built to facilitate transportation of people and goods. Many times, bridges were built at the site of mills or taverns. What follows is not a comprehensive list but a summary of some of the more notable sites.

HINKLETOWN

The first bridge across the Conestoga was a stone bridge built at Hinkletown in 1768 on the Paxton Highway, later called the Downingtown and Harrisburg Turnpike. The stone bridge remained in service until 1837, when it was replaced by a triple-span covered bridge. The covered bridge was 303 feet long and was 17 feet above the water. That bridge was replaced in 1896 by an iron and steel bridge with a plank driving surface. The iron bridge was in turn replaced by a steel bridge on concrete piers sometime before 1940. Finally, the steel bridge was replaced by a concrete bridge in the year 2000. There was a stone mill next to the bridge as early as 1797 on the site of an earlier log mill built by George Hinkle. The stone mill was rebuilt in 1830. The mill was demolished in 2000 to make room for a wider roadway when the new concrete bridge was constructed.

BINKLEY'S BRIDGE

The first stone arch bridge across the Conestoga, and possibly in the state, was built in 1789 by Christian Binkley and his wife, Elizabeth. Binkley built the bridge to provide access to his mill that he had built ten years earlier. The bridge was supported by ten stone arches. The mill and bridge were located just upstream from the place where the New Holland Pike crosses the river today. The area surrounding the mill and bridge became known collectively as Binkley's Bridge. Binkley nearly bankrupted himself in building the bridge, but he had no charter from the county to collect tolls, so some of his neighbors got together and raised funds to buy the bridge from Binkley on behalf of the county. The price paid for doing so was one thousand pounds in gold and silver coins, and it came with the stipulation that the bridge should be toll free forever.

Binkley's Bridge made it possible to charter the New Holland Turnpike in 1810. It ran from Blue Ball to the bridge and from the west side of the bridge to Lancaster. The bridge itself was not part of the turnpike's charter. Unfortunately, the bridge had a number of design flaws that caused it to succumb to the eroding effects of the elements, and it suffered a number of partial collapses that were repaired and finally completely collapsed after a flood in August 1867. Part of the reason that Binkley's Bridge collapsed was that it was not covered and did not have adequate drainage on the surface. Citizens immediately implored that the county rebuild the bridge. The county replaced the bridge with a covered bridge supported by stone arches in 1868 with the stipulation that the New Holland Turnpike Company provide one-third of the funds. The covered bridge was subsequently destroyed by fire in November 1882. Then in 1886, the county built a wrought-iron bridge at this location. By this time, the mill had been converted to a paper mill and was known as the Printer's Paper Mill. After a large truck failed to negotiate a sharp curve at the entrance of the bridge and damaged it, the roadway was relocated about a quarter mile downstream, and a new iron bridge carried the New Holland Pike over the river. That iron bridge has since been replaced by a concrete bridge.

Binkley's Bridge and Printer's Paper Mill. *Courtesy of LancasterHistory, Lancaster, Pennsylvania.*

WITMER'S BRIDGE

Abraham Witmer was a Huguenot and an agent for the London Land Company. He owned 150 acres of land about a mile east of the Conestoga where the Horseshoe Road intersects with the Philadelphia Road. Witmer's tavern still stands at that location. Following the Revolutionary War, Witmer

A History

moved to the west bank of the Conestoga, where he built a hotel on the site of an existing inn at the place where the Philadelphia Road crossed the river. The first inn was built around 1742. Witmer's hotel, completed in 1789, survives today as the Conestoga Inn and Restaurant.

In the fall of 1787, the state legislature passed an act for construction of a bridge across the Conestoga Creek and authorized Abraham Witmer to build the bridge and assess tolls. Witmer's first bridge was a wooden covered one. Tolls to cross the bridge were as follows:

- For every coach, landau, chariot, phaeton, wagon or other four-wheeled carriage, the sum of 1 shilling and 6 pence.
- For every chaise, riding chair, cart or other two-wheeled carriage, the sum of 9 pence.
- For every sled, the sum of 1 shilling.
- For every single horse and rider, the sum of 4 pence.
- For every foot passenger, the sum of 2 pence.
- For every head of horned cattle, sheep or swine, the sum of 1 penny.

Witmer's Bridge, circa 1887. *Courtesy of LancasterHistory, Lancaster, Pennsylvania.*

The Conestoga River

The first paved road in the United States opened in 1795 between Lancaster and Philadelphia. This road was made with crushed stones covered with gravel that raised the level of the road above the surrounding land and made it passable in all kinds of weather. This road design was patterned after the method developed by the Scotsman John McAdam. Stagecoach traffic between Lancaster and Philadelphia traveled on this road.

Then, in 1798, Witmer began the construction of a new, stone arch bridge. This bridge was 540 feet long and 19 feet wide and was constructed with nine arches. It opened for traffic in November 1800. Occasionally, it was told, some young Quakers would go into Lancaster for some entertainment and on their return journey would cross the bridge at full gallop without paying the toll. The next day, the fathers of the young men would be obliged to come to the bridge and pay the toll. Sometimes a wagoner would bypass the bridge to avoid paying the toll. If the wagon got stuck in the mud while crossing the river, Witmer would call them an "old stick in the mud!"[50]

Abraham Witmer died in 1818, and his brother David Witmer assumed ownership of the bridge. The county commissioners, with help from some

Inscription from Witmer's Bridge at Bridgeport.

private individuals, raised a sum of money to purchase the bridge from David Witmer. In 1827, the county paid $26,000 for the bridge, and it was declared free of tolls forever. A stone was placed in the center of the bridge with the following inscription:

> *Erected by Abraham Witmer,*
> *1799–1800,*
> *A Law of an Enlightened*
> *Commonwealth passed*
> *Apr. 4, 1798, sanctioned*
> *Thomas Mifflin, Governor,*
> *this Monument of the Public*
> *Spirit of an*
> *Individual*

Witmer's Bridge remained in service until 1933, when it was destroyed to make way for a new, wider bridge that could handle automobile traffic. The stone with the inscription may still be seen in the center of the new bridge.

ENGLESIDE

In 1806, Henry Slaymaker built a stone arch bridge over the Conestoga at the location of Graeff's Tavern south of Lancaster City. George Graeff built the two-story stone tavern in 1792. Prior to this, the Conestoga had to be crossed at Rock Ford, farther upstream. The addition of the bridge greatly increased the prosperity and importance of the tavern. Township elections were held for many years at the tavern. The stone bridge collapsed in 1824, and a temporary pontoon bridge was placed until a new bridge could be built. When the Marquis de Lafayette visited Lancaster in 1825, he had to cross the river on the pontoon bridge. Lafayette and his entourage arrived in four coach and fours, nearly swamping the bridge as they crossed.

A wooden covered bridge was completed in 1826. Later, Graeff's Tavern was rebranded as the Engleside Hotel, and the location at the end of South Prince Street became known as Engleside. The hotel included a small park. Ice skating was extremely popular during the winter months. Skaters could traverse the river from Engleside all the way up to Riegart's Landing. Graeff's landing on the south side of the river was one of the primary loading points for canalboats on the Conestoga Navigation slack-water canal during the mid-nineteenth century. Beginning service in 1891, a steamboat named the *Kangaroo* made regular trips from Engleside down the river to Levan's flour mill.

The covered bridge was dismantled in 1901, and a temporary ferry carried traffic across the river until a new iron bridge opened in the spring of 1902. The iron bridge was 306 feet wide and 24 feet wide and included room for team traffic, pedestrian traffic and a trolley line. The bridge had a macadam floor that needed to be replaced periodically throughout the next several decades. The old macadam floor of the bridge was finally replaced with a fabricated steel floor in 1949. People began calling it "the singing bridge" because of the sound that the tires made when crossing this floor.

As the towns south of the city became developed and traffic increased, the two-lane bridge became a bottleneck. A new bridge to carry the north-bound traffic on Willow Street Pike directly onto South Queen Street was completed in 1971. South-bound traffic still traveled over the old iron bridge. This situation was short-lived because in June 1972, Hurricane Agnes caused major flooding on the Conestoga that destroyed the northern span of the iron bridge. A temporary bridge was hastily put in place until a new bridge could be built. A new concrete and steel bridge opened for traffic in 1975. The venerable Engleside Hotel today is called the Distelfink Inn, and the tavern operates as the Dirty Ol' Tavern.

CONESTOGA CREEK VIADUCT

When the Pennsylvania Canal commissioners determined that it would not be feasible to build a canal from Philadelphia to Columbia on the Susquehanna, they decided to build a railroad on that portion of the main line instead. As a result, the Canal Commission formed the Philadelphia and Columbia Railroad (P&CR). A wooden railroad bridge was built across the Conestoga in 1829 to carry the railroad. The bridge was 1,412 feet long and constructed of eleven wooden lattice trusses. The P&CR opened for business in 1834. The railroad and canal system reduced the time required to ship goods from Philadelphia to Pittsburgh from the twenty-three days it took by Conestoga wagon down to just four.

The Pennsylvania Railroad (PRR) purchased the P&CR in 1857 and made it part of its main line. The PRR shortened the length of the bridge

A HISTORY

An Amtrak train crosses the Conestoga Creek Viaduct as it approaches Lancaster Station.

and replaced the wooden trusses with iron ones in 1863. Then in 1888, the PRR began construction of a stone arch bridge across the river. The bridge was intended to be wide enough for four tracks, but only half that width was completed. The new stone arch Conestoga Creek Viaduct opened for traffic in 1889. On February 20, 1960, a mail train derailed while crossing the Conestoga Creek Viaduct. Sixteen cars of a twenty-five-car train were derailed, with two of them landing in the water. Thousands of pieces of mail were scattered and soaked in the wreck. East- and westbound traffic on the main line was rerouted for several hours until the tracks were cleared.

IRON BRIDGE

The Iron Bridge on Iron Bridge Road was built in 1898. A plaque near the bridge states the following: "The Iron Bridge Road Bridge is one of the oldest remaining pin-connected Pratt truss highway bridges in Lancaster County. It was built for the total cost of $1,767.00. Farmers heavily crossed

The Conestoga River

Iron Bridge on Iron Bridge Road.

the bridge which originally was built with a plank flooring that was repaired in 1926. The pin-connected truss system was popular for use with local roads in Pennsylvania from the 1880s–1910."

COVERED BRIDGES

Oberholtzer's Mill Covered Bridge, also known as the Wabank Covered Bridge, the Third Lock Bridge or Big Conestoga #22, was built in 1835 to span the Conestoga south of Millersville. Rebuilt in 1841, this bridge was a double-span, wooden arch covered bridge. Isaac Heiney built a gristmill here in 1807. The mill was sold to the Wabank Company in 1845, which, in turn, sold it to Daniel Oberholtzer. The eastern span of this bridge collapsed in 1962, and the western span collapsed in 1969. The piers for this bridge are still visible at the end of Short Lane.

The first bridge at Safe Harbor was a covered bridge built by John Black in 1838. That bridge was blown apart by a violent windstorm in 1866 and was subsequently rebuilt only to be washed away in 1870. Elias McMellen returned the bridge to its site and returned it to service. The bridge was washed away again in 1873. McMellen built another two-span covered bridge in its place that was fifteen feet above the water. That bridge was destroyed by the great ice flood in March 1904. By the end of 1904, an iron truss bridge was put into service, supported by new stone abutments. The iron bridge was replaced with the current steel and concrete bridge in 1988. This is the bridge that carries River Road across the Conestoga just below the remains of lock #8.

The Slackwater Covered Bridge was built in 1839. It was a double-span bridge, 269 feet long. Later known as the Shober's Paper Mill bridge, it was replaced in 1957. The piers are still visible next to the new bridge. The new bridge has obliterated all signs of the mill.

Bushong's Mill Covered Bridge, also known as Elmer Zook's Mill Bridge, was built in 1843 by Joseph Elliot and Robert Russell. At 195 feet long with a clear span of 180 feet, this was the longest single-span covered bridge in the county. The covered bridge was dismantled and replaced with the current steel and concrete span in 1952. This bridge spans the river at Quarry Road/Bushong Road next to Bushong's Mill.

Hunsecker's Mill Covered Bridge was built in 1843 by John Russell. At 180 feet, it is the longest single-span covered bridge in the county. Destroyed in 1972 by Hurricane Agnes, it has since been rebuilt. The original cost to build was $1,988. In 1973, it was rebuilt for $321,302. Constructed as a single-span, double–Burr arch truss[51] design, this bridge has horizontal floorboards, which give it a unique feel as you drive across. It is interesting that on one side of the bridge, the road is called Hunsecker Road, while on the other side it is called Hunsicker Road. This bridge is in Manheim Township.

Bitzer's Mill Covered Bridge, also known as Eberly's Cider Mill Bridge, was built in 1846 by George Fink and Sam Reamsnyder. Located on Cider Mill Road in West Earl Township, it is ninety-eight feet long and fifteen feet wide and is the oldest bridge in the county still in use. The bridge is a single span Burr arch truss design. The bridge was reconstructed in 1997. The superstructure was damaged in 2015 when someone attempted to drive an oversized vehicle through it. The bridge has since been repaired.

The Conestoga River

The 1843 Hunsecker's Mill Covered Bridge.

Bitzer's Mill/Eberly's Cider Mill Covered Bridge.

A History

Umble's Mill Covered Bridge crossed the river in the town of Eden just south of the New Holland Turnpike at Umble's Mill, also known as the Eden Roller Mill. The 158-foot-long bridge was built by Israel Groff in 1848. During the time when Binkley's Bridge was being repaired, traffic on the New Holland Pike was diverted across this bridge. The bridge was replaced with a concrete bridge in 1962. The 1962 bridge was replaced in 2019.

Snavely's Mill Covered Bridge, also known as the Second Lock Covered Bridge, was built at the location of the second navigation lock in 1857. The road that crossed the bridge became known as Second Lock Road. This bridge was burned by vandals in 1968 and was never rebuilt. The piers are still visible at the end of Second Lock Road.

Poole Forge closed in 1852 with the decline of the iron industry. In 1858, a group of citizens signed a petition for Lancaster County to build a covered bridge across the Conestoga Creek at Poole Forge. The bridge was constructed in 1859 by Levi Fink and Elias McMellen at the location where the Downingtown and Ephrata Turnpike crossed the Conestoga. The bridge is a single-span, double–Burr truss design that measures ninety-nine feet long and fifteen feet wide. Today, Poole Forge is open to the public as a park and is a popular venue for outdoor weddings.

Poole Forge Covered Bridge.

The Conestoga River

Iron Bridge at Rock Hill.

The Rock Hill Covered Bridge was built in 1858 by Jacob Peters. It was a two-span bridge measuring 273 feet. It was replaced by a steel bridge with high trusses built in 1923. The bridge is 256 feet long with two spans.

The Old Factory Bridge crossed the river at the end of South Duke Street, Lancaster at Sunnyside. The first bridge on this site, built in 1853, was an open, two-span, wooden bridge with arches. This bridge was replaced by a covered bridge built by Elias McMellen in 1867. It was a two-span bridge that measured just over 210 feet long. The Old Factory Bridge was in service for eighty-one years until it was replaced by the current steel and concrete bridge in 1948.

The New Danville Covered Bridge spanned the river about 380 feet upstream of the current concrete bridge that carries the New Danville Pike. The two-span covered bridge was built around 1864 and was destroyed by fire in 1928. The center abutment is still standing in the middle of the river.

Kurtz's Mill Bridge, also known as Isaac Bear's Mill, was built in 1876 by W.W. Upp with a single-span, double–Burr arch truss design and is ninety-four feet long and fifteen feet wide. This bridge once spanned the

A History

Kurtz's Mill Bridge in Lancaster County Park.

Weaver's Mill Covered Bridge.

The Conestoga River

Pinetown Covered Bridge.

Conestoga on Kurtz Road but was washed downriver in 1972 by Hurricane Agnes. In 1975, it was moved to Lancaster County Park, where it spans the Mill Creek.

Located at the site of a former sawmill, Weaver's Mill Covered Bridge, also known as Shearer's Mill Bridge, was built in 1878 by B.C. Carter and J.F. Stauffer. It is eighty-five feet long and fifteen feet wide, constructed as a single-span, double–Burr arch truss design. The bridge is on Weaverland Road in Caernarvon Township, not far from Goodville.

Pinetown Covered Bridge, also known as Nolt's Point Mill Bridge, is located where the Lititz Run enters the Conestoga. The Henry Leman Rifle Factory was located a short distance upstream of this bridge. This is a county bridge and is designated as Big Conestoga #6. The bridge was built in 1897 by Elias McMellen. It is a single-span, double–Burr truss design that measures 133 feet long and 15 feet wide. It was destroyed by Hurricane Agnes in 1972 but rebuilt soon after. The bridge was repaired a second time after it sustained damage from Tropical Storm Lee in 2011.

See Appendix B for a complete list of bridges.

A History

MILLS

Lancaster County's mills were an extremely important part of the commerce of the county in the early days. An 1840 census showed 383 mills in the county, which amounts to 1 mill for every two and a half square miles. They were hubs of the local economy. Today, they stand as testaments to a bygone era. Several of the mills in the county are set up as museums and are worth a visit. Most notable is the Mascot Mill on the Mill Stream south of Leola. You can tour the mill and learn about this part of Lancaster's history.

Spring (Zug's/Grube's) Mill is located along Red School Road south of Route 23 just outside Morgantown. The present mill was built in 1823 by David Zug. It replaced an earlier mill that was built in 1753. The water source was a mountain spring (hence the name "Spring Mill"). The mill used an overshot wheel and the outflow drained into the Conestoga River. Milling operations ceased in 1923. The mill is now used as part of a furniture business.

In 1845, David Longnecker and John F. Steinman formed the Conestoga Cotton Mills Company. Mill #1 was completed in 1846, and operations began with six thousand spindles and 216 looms in March 1847. Mill #2

The 1823 Spring Mill.

opened in August 1849 with eight thousand spindles and 288 looms. In 1851, mill #3 opened with ten thousand spindles and 264 looms.[52] The Conestoga Navigation system was instrumental in supplying coal as fuel for these steam-driven mills. The panic of 1857 caused several of the mills to close. Mills 1 and 2 were sold at sheriff's sale to Francis Schroder and Company, which operated the mills until at least 1883. By that time, a railroad line was extended down Water Street, and the canal was no longer needed for supplying fuel and raw materials or for shipping finished goods.

In August 1848, the Safe Harbor Iron Works opened for business. Reeves, Abbot & Company chose the Safe Harbor area because of the availability of iron ore nearby and for its proximity to the canals on both the Conestoga and the nearby Susquehanna. The primary product was railroad iron used by the Pennsylvania Railroad Company. The works consisted of a blast furnace, foundry and rolling mill. The works primarily produced railroad iron but also manufactured wrought-iron cannon that were used by the Union army in the latter part of the Civil War. The works were in operation until 1865, when the crib dam across the Susquehanna was destroyed, which cut off its means of transportation.[53]

The ironworks remained idle until 1879, when the company built a short railroad branch for the purpose of connecting the works with the Columbia and Port Deposit Railroad, which ran along the Susquehanna. The works at that time were producing puddle iron for the Phoenix Iron Company in Phoenixville. In 1882, the plant produced ten thousand tons of puddled iron. Operations ceased in 1883. The plant remained idle for about ten years when it reopened as a factory to produce blue-tipped, phosphorous matches. In its heyday, Safe Harbor boasted many hotels, liquor stores and beer parlors, earning its reputation as the booziest town in the county. On March 8, 1904, an ice floe on the Susquehanna jammed just below the outlet of the Conestoga River, causing a major ice flood on the Conestoga. Most of the buildings in Safe Harbor Village were heavily damaged or destroyed. The flood caused damage as far upstream as Slackwater. The town at Safe Harbor lingered while the low-grade railroad was being constructed but became a ghost town after the construction was completed. The remaining buildings were razed around 1907. The Safe Harbor Trestle was built in 1905. It is a steel truss trestle that carried the Atglen and Susquehanna ("Low Grade") branch of the Pennsylvania Railroad over the Conestoga at Safe Harbor. Now abandoned, the tracks were removed in 1990.

A History

The Safe Harbor Trestle.

Bitzer's (Eberly's) Cider Mill is on Cider Mill Road right next to the covered bridge. The date of construction of this mill is unclear, but John Bitzer owned it in 1864. The mill was used variously as a gristmill, flour mill, sawmill and cider mill. Nathan Eberly owned it when it closed in 1933. The mill dam still exists.

The Eden Roller Mill is located on Millcross Road near the town of Eden. The current mill was built circa 1870 on a site that had earlier mills. Two turbines drove the mill. There was a fulling mill on this site in 1812 that was converted to a carding mill in 1824. A paper mill operated on the site in 1864. The current brick mill was used as a flour/gristmill until it closed sometime in the early twentieth century.

The Brownstown (Wolf's) Mill was built in 1856 by Jacob and Lavina Wolf. This mill is located on West Farmersville Road just across the river from the town of Brownstown. The current mill replaced an earlier stone mill that was built on this site in 1750. A log mill was located on this site as early as 1730. Two turbines drove the mill, which had a capacity of seventy-five barrels per day. Milling operations ended in 1929. Today, the mill is a private residence.

Eden Roller Mill.

The 1856 Brownstown Mill.

A HISTORY

The 1857 Bushong's Mill.

Bushong's (Zook's) Mill is located on the south side of Quarry Road. Built in 1857 by John and Elizabeth Bushong, the mill operated as a grist- and sawmill through 1920. The original mill used an overshot wheel. In 1920, two turbines were installed in place of the overshot wheel, and the mill was converted to a roller mill. Elmer Zook took ownership of the mill in the 1930s and operated it until 1972 (Hurricane Agnes). Beginning in 1974 and continuing until at least 2006, the mill was used to grind flour for the pretzel industry.

The Spring Grove (Oberholtzer's/Horst Bros.) Mill was built in 1868 by Jacob and Catherine Oberholtzer. The mill is located on Spring Grove Road in East Earl Township. The mill was powered by two turbines and could produce twenty barrels of flour per day. Milling operations continued until about 1987. The dam on the Conestoga is still present. The mill, which is in a state of disrepair, is used for equipment storage.

On November 7, 1872, Samuel Reeves sold the upper half of the Conestoga Navigation System from Reigart's Landing to the outlet of lock #4 at the southern end of the canal at Petersville in Conestoga Township to Jacob G. Peters and George Levan.[54] The United States Post Office lists the location

The Conestoga River

Levan's Flour Mill. *Courtesy of LancasterHistory, Lancaster, Pennsylvania.*

at the intersection of Slackwater Road and Stehman Road as Petersville. In other words, Petersville was where the village of Slackwater is today. Then in December of that year, Peters sold his half interest of the portion between Reigart's Landing and lock #1 to George Levan. Levan built a large flour mill across the river from lock #1.

According to the *American Miller*, George Levan built his mill in 1870. The mill was operated as a fulling mill at first. It was a four-story brick building and at the time was the largest fulling mill in the county. In 1879, the fulling mill was dismantled, and the entire building was used to produce flour. A narrow-gauge railroad bridge was constructed across the river to connect with the Pennsylvania Railroad. George Levan also served on the building committee of the Millersville Normal School. After George's death, his two sons, Landis and Samuel, continued the operation as Levan & Sons. The mill was destroyed by fire on June 28, 1913.[55]

The Slackwater Burr Mill was built by Tobias Stehman in approximately 1805. Later, ownership was transferred to Christian Rohrer and then to Abraham Peters. John Shober purchased the mill in 1866 and converted it to a paper mill. The paper mill at Petersville/Slackwater was used to

A History

High water flows over the dam at Bushong's Mill.

manufacture paper for books and newsprint from rags. The rags were boiled in alkali under pressure and reduced to pulp, which was then made into paper. The buildings formed a hollow square, with the open side facing the road between Slackwater and Millersville. The mill was powered by five water turbines augmented by two steam boilers. The mill employed forty workers and in 1882 was producing four tons of paper per day.[56]

While the mills were an essential element of the local economy during the eighteenth and nineteenth centuries, their dams and ponds completely altered the ecology of the county. The mills were often close enough together that the water in the pond behind each dam would back up all the way to the next higher dam. The dams collected sediment over time that built up in some places as deep as fifteen feet. Later, when the dams were destroyed, all that sediment began to wash down the river into the Susquehanna and ultimately to the bay. During periods of high-water flow due to an event like a hurricane, the sediment plume in the upper part of the bay is visible from satellite.

See Appendix C for a complete list of mill sites.

Chapter 5

STEAM AND ELECTRICITY

The Victorian era marked a time of tremendous growth and change. Improvements in steam power enabled that technology to be employed in many ways. The railroads, of course, were steam powered, but also factories were built using steam as a power source. Even the city water plant augmented its water wheels with steam pumps. As the rural population grew, new bridges were needed to provide access to the mills and to bring goods to market. Electricity was introduced to the city for lighting at first and later to power the public trolley system. And the Victorians loved their leisure time. Resorts and hotels were popular, along with theaters and roller skating, as well as boating and swimming in the summer and ice skating in the winter.

> *Lancaster city enjoys almost unequalled advantages of location in many respects. She sits on an elevated limestone ridge, which secures her the advantage of excellent health and satisfactory drainage. Along her eastern and southern borders winds one of the most beautiful rivers to be seen anywhere, affording visions of picturesque scenery and beauty excelled nowhere, as I believe, on this continent. Around her, beyond her own territorial limits, is spread a country than which the sun in his course shines on none richer or more beautiful, and which vies with the garden spots of the world. Take along with these the general aggregate of her population, in intelligence, in industry, in wealth, and, may I not add, in morals, and we have an aggregation of conditions and circumstances of the most desirable kind, and which, all things considered, make her one of the most desirable places on the globe to be born, live and die in.*
>
> —*Frank R. Diffenderffer*

A History

WABANK HOUSE

In the 1850s, a group of twenty gentlemen from Lancaster City decided that Lancaster could use a resort. Rather than having to travel to the mountains or the seashore for relaxation, why not build a place somewhere nearby overlooking the beautiful Conestoga? There was at that time an old tavern on the banks of the Conestoga that was a favorite place to get away for some revelry. The men believed that would be a great location for a resort, so these gentlemen formed a stock company and sold forty shares of stock at $1,000 per share. To find a name for their venture, they advertised their intentions and offered a prize of $25 to the person who submitted a name that the committee preferred. The winning entry was Wabank, suggested by Mrs. Mathiot, Christopher Hager's daughter and the wife of one of the shareholders. The name was chosen because they thought it had a Native American ring to it.

On January 3, 1854, the Wabank House Company purchased two tracts of land at lock #3 of the Conestoga Navigation Company, which included the old tavern, several mills and a miller's house and approximately sixteen acres of land. By the end of the year, construction was underway, employing twenty-three carpenters at a rate of eighty-seven and a half cents per day. The construction costs exceeded the estimates, as these projects usually do, and the total cost came to about $60,000. Construction was completed in the summer of 1855, and Mrs. Ann Haines of Donegal was hired to run the establishment. The house had four stories and an attic and measured 105 feet long and 45 feet wide. It had one hundred rooms and a dining room that could seat three hundred persons. Forty "colored" waiters were employed to serve the many guests. The entire structure was surrounded with wide verandas on the first, second and third floors.

The hotel was opened with a "hop," which was attended by a large crowd of people from the city. The Wabank House was an immensely popular destination for family picnics and vacations. The Lancaster Bar held a five-dollar-per-plate banquet for the State Supreme Court. The State Medical Society met there for its annual sessions. President Buchanan visited on at least one occasion. In September 1858, several companies of soldiers camped there in what was called "Camp Conestoga." About one hundred tents were pitched on the grounds, and over two thousand persons attended the grand review on September 30. The Wabank was known for its sumptuous fare, especially the catfish and waffle suppers.

In spite of its seemingly great popularity, the hotel was not profitable. Mrs. Haines had left the establishment, and the house was managed by William T. Youart, who also ran the Exchange Hotel on the square in Lancaster. The Medical Society began to hold its annual meeting elsewhere, and there were fewer customers from the city. The mill and other properties not related to the hotel were sold to the miller Daniel Overholtzer in 1855. The board listed the hotel property for sale in 1857, but there were no takers. The company went into foreclosure, and the hotel came into the possession of Mr. Overholtzer. Overholtzer sold the hotel building to Samuel Lichtenthaler of Lititz in 1863 for $4,000. Youart went on to become the proprietor of the Engleside Hotel at Graeff's Landing, which he managed for sixteen years.

Lichtenthaler was the owner of the Lititz Springs Hotel. He disassembled the Wabank House and transported it to Lititz. It took one hundred four-horse wagonloads to transport it. Lichtenthaler reconstructed the hotel on the square of Lititz adjacent to the Lititz Springs Hotel. The two buildings were connected by a corridor and were together known as the Lititz Springs Hotel. The new addition opened on July 4, 1864. The hotel operated at that location for a decade until it was destroyed by fire on July 31, 1873. The fire brigade was able to save the older part of the hotel.[57] The Lititz Springs Hotel was renamed the General Sutter Inn in 1930 in honor of John Sutter, who lived his final years in Lititz. In 2020, after more information came to light about John Sutter's practice of enslaving Native Americans, the proprietor rebranded the hotel back to its former name. It once again operates as the Lititz Springs Hotel and Spa.

ROCKY SPRINGS

No treatise of the Conestoga River would be complete without mentioning Rocky Springs Park. Rocky Springs played a major part in the social fabric of Lancaster City and County for nearly a century.

In 1855, a Lancaster butcher named Michael Trissler purchased land along the Conestoga Creek and built the Rocky Springs Hotel. The hotel was in operation until 1876. During this time, the grounds were used for picnics by families, churches and local organizations. The hotel building still stands and is now a bed-and-breakfast. In 1882, Samuel J. Demuth purchased Rocky Springs from the Trissler estate. Demuth owned a confectionery in the city at 7 East King Street. For a time, the park was named Demuth Park and was one of the best picnic areas of the

A History

Postcard from Rocky Springs on the "Conestoga Creek." *Author's collection.*

time. Demuth enlarged the park with the addition of fourteen acres of land adjoining the original estate. After Demuth died in 1888, his family continued to operate the park as a picnic ground.

In 1890, John B. Peoples leased the park for five years. Peoples added various amusements, picnic tables, benches and a goldfish-filled fountain at the entrance. At this time, the first *Lady Gay*, a small side-wheeled steamboat, began to carry people to and from the park. By 1894, Peoples had added bathing houses near the creek and created a sandy beach. Hundreds of people were visiting the park by this time. In 1896, the park was leased to Herman B. Griffiths and Emma J. Wiener from Philadelphia.

In 1899, Rocky Springs was sold to Thomas Rees of Pittsburgh, and Herman Griffiths was retained as the manager. Griffiths moved into the mansion house with his wife, Emma, and two children, Isabella and William. Griffiths added a steam merry-go-round and dance pavilion and replaced the park's coal oil lamps with electric lights.

During the years from 1899 to 1918, the Christian & Missionary Alliance held its missions conferences at Rocky Springs for a full week each summer. As many as ten thousand people were on the grounds for these services. People were baptized in the Conestoga River. There was a field of one hundred tents and dormitories for men and women. In 1908, the mission's offering was over $51,000.

The Conestoga River

The Conestoga Traction Company began trolley service to the park on May 10, 1903. There was a two-line track that ran from the city down through the Sunnyside Peninsula. As many as twenty cars were in service during peak times. A two-thousand-seat theater was built in 1904 to host vaudeville and variety shows. This was eventually torn down during World War II, and the materials were used to support the war effort. In 1907, a four-hundred-foot-long roller-skating rink was constructed. In 1918, the Jack Rabbit roller coaster was built. This coaster featured a five-hundred-foot tunnel.

In 1921, the Crystal Pool opened. The pool measured 80 by 140 feet with two diving boards plus a wading pool and bathhouse. In 1924, the Carousel house was built, and a new Dentzel carousel was installed with forty-eight hand-carved animals and two chariots. About this time, a young man named Joseph Figari began working at the park selling shaved ice with flavored syrup drizzled over it at the concession stand. In 1928, the Jack Rabbit coaster was dismantled, and the Wildcat was built. The Wildcat had a 90-foot, sixty-degree drop and a 500-foot tunnel. Joe Figari purchased the park from Herman Griffith in 1935.

CONESTOGA PARK

Conestoga Park was located on the west side of the river just below Witmer's Bridge. In 1890, David Burkholder laid out a driveway along the Conestoga that was called the Conestoga Boulevard. The boulevard was a mile and a third in length and was designed for driving horses and carriages for pleasure rides. Racing and bicycles were prohibited. A large pavilion was erected the following year. The boulevard officially opened for business in 1895. The Pennsylvania Traction Company, as it was called at that time, provided transportation from the city to the park with a loading platform near the pavilion. The park was popular for picnics, and rowboats were available for boating on the Conestoga. Regattas were held regularly, for which boat owners would decorate their crafts and thousands of people lined both sides of the riverbank cheering for their favorite.

The pavilion, known as the Conestoga Park Theatre, was the site of many performances, including one by John Philip Sousa. The theater was three-sided with a stage at the north end. Admission was five cents. The theater was destroyed in 1902 when a freak lightning bolt struck, causing a fire. The park

A HISTORY

View of the Conestoga River south of Witmer's Bridge, showing the *Lady Gay* boathouse, the *Lady Gay* paddleboat and the Conestoga Park Theater. *Courtesy of LancasterHistory, Lancaster, Pennsylvania.*

languished for about a decade until Howard Doan purchased the property. Doan built a new pavilion that was larger than the first and included a dance floor. He also added a $10,000 carousel and laid out walks and benches throughout the park. The new Conestoga Park opened to the public on Memorial Day 1915. Unfortunately, the new pavilion was destroyed by an arsonist in January 1916.

PEOPLE'S BATHING RESORT

John Peoples purchased land directly across the river from Rocky Springs, where he built his own resort. People's Bathing Resort was located about a mile below Conestoga Park. It opened in 1896 and was a popular facility for swimming and boating. A toboggan (that is, a water slide) located at the northern end of the park provided thrills for the more adventurous. The

The Conestoga River

People's Bathing Resort postcard. *Author's collection.*

resort included a skating rink that was alleged to be the largest in the county. A miniature electric railway provided transportation between the resort and Conestoga Park.

LANCASTER'S NAVY

The *Lady Gay* was a steam-powered pleasure boat that was built by "Captain" John B. Peoples in 1890 at Conestoga Park. The *Lady Gay* was patterned after a ferryboat that operated on the Susquehanna between Wrightsville and Columbia at the time. Its name was a nod to the wife of engineer E.F. Gay, who designed the Conestoga Slackwater Canal. The *Lady Gay* was seventy-five feet long with a beam of nineteen feet. A twelve-horsepower steam engine was installed initially, but after ten years, the power plant was upgraded to twenty horsepower. For the first six years, the *Lady Gay* ran between a wharf at Conestoga Park just below the bridge down to Rocky Springs, which was managed by Captain Peoples at the time. The *Lady Gay* had a capacity of 375 people and could make the round trip in about thirty minutes. The fastest time between Conestoga Park and Rocky Springs was clocked at nine minutes.

A History

Navigating the river required skill and knowledge, as the draft at Conestoga Park was only two feet. This increased to near fifteen feet above the City Mill dam. The *Lady Gay* made twenty round trips per day, with the final trip being billed as a "moonlight cruise."

Two other boats, the *Evelyn B.* and the *Emma Belle*, were built by Herman Griffiths at Rocky Springs in 1896. These boats had a capacity of six hundred people and could navigate with only sixteen inches of draft. They were eighty feet long with a twenty-foot beam and were twenty feet high from the waterline to the top of the pilot's house. They each had a fifty-horsepower engine that drove stern paddle wheels. The *Evelyn B.* or *Emma Belle* left Conestoga park every fifteen minutes. The round-trip fare was ten cents.

In the summer of 1900, Peoples discounted the round-trip fare on the *Lady Gay* from Conestoga Park to his new bathing resort to half price (five cents). Peoples also operated a free ferry between his resort and Rocky Springs for anyone who wanted to cross. The manager of Rocky Springs, Emma Wiener, sued Peoples for trespassing and accused him of persuading passengers to ride his boat instead of the one to Rocky Springs. The case was dismissed because the swimming dock that Peoples used to transfer passengers was in the Conestoga and was therefore deemed to be public property. The court

The *Emma Belle* paddleboat built at Rocky Springs in 1896. *Courtesy of LancasterHistory, Lancaster, Pennsylvania.*

The Conestoga River

The *Evelyn B.* paddleboat operated on the Conestoga between Witmer's Bridge and Rocky Springs Park. *Courtesy of LancasterHistory, Lancaster, Pennsylvania.*

also noted that the landings at Conestoga Park were clearly marked as to their destinations.

In 1902, a storm caused a large flood on the Conestoga. The *Evelyn B.* and *Emma Belle* were both swept off their moorings. The *Lady Gay* remained chained to its wharf. The *Emma Belle* managed to be saved by a rope thrown from the shore, but the *Evelyn B.* was carried over the City Mill dam and crashed into the Poor House Bridge below the dam. The pilot was unable to save the boat and just managed to save his life by abandoning ship just above the dam. The boat was destroyed along with a "floating bath house" that had also been carried down the stream from Rocky Springs.[58]

On May 10, 1903, the Conestoga Traction Company opened a trolley line to Rocky Springs Park. This signaled the end of the Conestoga Navy. The *Emma Belle* was put on dry dock and dismantled. People's Bathing Resort had to close because the water in the Conestoga was polluted by sewage and was unfit for bathing. The *Lady Gay* made its last voyage in 1915, after which it was beached at the City Mill. Shortly after, it was accidentally destroyed by fire.

A History

ELECTRIC POWER GENERATION

Incorporated on February 2, 1897, the Lancaster Electric, Heat & Power Company acquired the canal rights and property at Wabank, Slackwater and Rock Hill. The Slackwater and Rock Hill dams were converted to produce hydroelectric power at this time. The plant at Wabank was put into service in 1901. The electricity was used to light the city with electric arc lighting that hung from wires above the streets and to power the trolleys of the Conestoga Traction Company.

In 1913, the Lancaster Power Company was split into several companies by township. On May 13, the Buchanan Water and Power Company was chartered to supply power to Lancaster Township, having its source of supply at Wabank. On the same day, the Lafayette Water and Power Company was chartered to supply power to Pequea Township using the same source. The dam at Wabank was 280 feet in length and about 15 feet high, and the water backed up to the second lock mill. The plant had no headrace but a large, triangular forebay, formed by a heavy masonry wall with four steel gates. Three forty-eight-inch turbines rated at eighty horsepower each powered a 175-kilowatt generator. The plant operated eighteen hours per day.[59] The Wabank plant burned down in November 1917.

The Slackwater plant was rebuilt in 1910. Then, on June 9, 1913, the Lancaster County Power and Water Company formed, with its source of power being the Slackwater plant.[60] The dam was a timber-crib structure about 335 feet long with sluice gates at its southern end. Water backed up 6.4 miles to the Wabank dam. The old canal was utilized as a headrace. The headrace was about 1,300 feet long and had a cross-section similar to that of canals at that date. The old canal was provided with mechanically operated steel head gates and two substantial timber cribs for ice protection, and 5,700 volts of power were transmitted to the Engleside Station of the Edison Electric Illuminating Company of Lancaster. Remnants of the canal can still be seen today around the area where the power plant was located. The dam was destroyed by a flood in 1946.

The Rock Hill power plant was also reconstructed in 1910. The dam was a timber-crib structure 240 feet long and 12 feet high. A 200-foot headrace was formed by a masonry wall parallel to the hillside and was provided with steel gates operated with overhead chain blocks. The turbines were in a deep pit, excavated in solid rock, 28 feet below the level of the tail race. Two turbines powered a generator that produced 5,700 volts of three-phase current.[61]

Slackwater power plant. *Courtesy of LancasterHistory, Lancaster, Pennsylvania.*

Two power companies operated at Rock Hill: the Hamilton Water & Power Company supplied power for Manor Township, and the Stevens Water & Power Company supplied power for Conestoga Township. Both power companies were chartered on May 13, 1913. Operations ceased in 1946. The remains of the power plant (presumably built on top of the old lock) are still visible. There is a plaque mounted on the side of the old sluice gate honoring local fisherman James R. Kilby, who gave his life on May 15, 1989, while attempting to rescue some canoers who got hung up on the remains of the dam. The dam has since been destroyed.

Chapter 6
CONSERVATION

In the nineteenth century, the priorities were to utilize the natural resources for the maximum benefit of commercial and industrial concerns. There was little or no consideration of the ecological impacts of constricting the water flow. Many dams were built on the river to generate the water power required for all kinds of milling operations. Sawmills, gristmills, fulling mills, roller mills, water pumps—all were powered by water before, and even during, the steam era. Later, the dams were used to generate electric power. The dams were located, and their heights selected, such that the water behind each dam would back up to the next higher dam. This converted the river into a series of connected ponds.

The dams made the river deeper, which caused the river to also become much wider. The waterlines in the late 1800s were much different than they are today. This can be seen especially at lock #8 in Safe Harbor Park, where the lock is quite far away from the river as it now flows. Runoff from agriculture filled the river with topsoil and fertilizer (both the natural and the chemical kind). The amount of runoff from land used for agriculture is twice the amount that was generated by forested land. The arrested water flow at the head of each dam caused the sediments that were naturally carried by the river to settle out above the dams. This sediment piled up over the years until the sediment stacks became many feet deep. The layer of sediment above the dam at the waterworks was over nine feet. Aggravating the situation was the common habit of using the river as a dump for garbage and sewage. All this material would become trapped at the head of each dam.

THE CONESTOGA RIVER

SEWAGE TREATMENT

Raw sewage was another major problem. Sewage entered the river at various points along the river, especially near the city of Lancaster. Lancaster City, like many older cities, has a combined sewer system where storm runoff and household sewage are mixed in the same system. This water was all returned to the river in three main sewer outfalls and two smaller ones. The dam at Levan's Mill, about a mile below the city, prevented the sewage from flowing out of the city area. Between Prince Street and Levan's Mill on low flow days, the river water contained about one-fifth raw sewage. The bottom of the stream was covered with a heavy deposit of sewage sludge. The river would be covered in foam on wash days. It was claimed that the area below the Rock Hill dam smelled like dirty wash water one hundred yards away from the river.

In the early twentieth century, pleas began to be heard to clean up the river. In 1906, the commissioner of health decreed that a dam be built below the intake of the city waterworks to prevent contaminated water from backing up into the water supply. In June 1908, the commissioner granted permission for the discharge of raw sewage into the Conestoga until July 1, 1911, provided that the city would submit detailed plans for the construction of sewage treatment plants for the entire city.[62] The city did not comply with the provision. In 1912, the city council created a special sewage disposal commission to study the question of sewage disposal. No definite plans were prepared, so in 1916, the commissioner again urged the city to abate the pollution of the river by sewage from the city. Then World War I intervened, and all action was postponed.

An article in the *Lancaster New Era* on January 3, 1920, stated, "The stream with its possibilities for beauty, pleasure, usefulness, and healthfulness is now relatively unused, largely by reason of the discharge of the city's raw sewage into it. Proper sewage treatment is urgently needed to remedy the present situation and is the first step toward making Conestoga Creek a valuable asset to the community." The city put forward a plan to sell bonds in the amount of $825,000, approximately half of which was designated to build a sewage disposal system. The rest of the money was to go to street improvements and a public comfort station. The city held a special election on the referendum in May. The measure was voted down by a margin of three to one, prompting the state to declare that it would build the sewage system and send the bill to the city. The state did not follow through on that threat.

A History

On November 6, 1920, a writer in the *Lancaster Intelligencer* stated:

> *The matter of the proposed boulevard along the Conestoga creek from the end of South Queen street to the city water works is generally considered a matter of extravagance which can wait until more essential needs have been given attention. The consensus of opinion appears to be that this matter should not be given serious attention until the sewage problem has been settled and the ill-smelling stream of filth that now pollutes the stream is eliminated.*

During the next decade and a half, there were many pleas and arguments on the urgent need for a solution to the city's sewage problem. The Lancaster Chamber, in its 1924 bulletin, listed "Boulevard and Parks along the Conestoga" in its program of work; however, there was little point in making parks while the river ran polluted by sewage. In 1929, city planner John Nolan presented a comprehensive plan for a "Greater Lancaster." The "Nolan Plan" suggested reserving recreation space along the river and urged steps to clean up the raw sewage pouring into the river.[63] The February 1931 bulletin of the Lancaster Chamber included the headline, "What Shall It Be—Scenic Beauty or Open Sewer?"

Finally, in October 1932, plans for two sewage plants were presented to city council. The North Plant would be built on the Ranck farm east of the city and the South Plant on the site of the old power plant at Engleside. Bids were accepted, and construction began the following year. The North Plant began operating at the end of 1934, while the South Plant began operations in early 1935. At last, a major source of pollution in the river was mitigated. The system had the capacity to fully process the sewage load during normal water flow. But owing to the nature of Lancaster's combined sewer system, the plants were overwhelmed during periods of heavy rain, at which times raw sewage would still make its way into the river. Work on the proposed parks and scenic boulevard was postponed during World War II, when all attention went to the war effort.

CONESTOGA VALLEY ASSOCIATION

In 1946, a new comprehensive plan for the city, known as the Baker Plan, was presented. It again urged that a scenic drive with open space be built along the river front. The Lancaster wartime Salvage Committee was actively promoting the Conestoga Boulevard with parks, open space and a convention hall as a desirable "veterans of all wars memorial."[64] In July of that year, Ira H. Landis offered a one-and-a-half-mile tract of land where the Conestoga Park had been located along the Conestoga to the city at no cost as a seed to start the Boulevard project. Lancaster civic leaders held a public meeting in September 1946 to discuss the offer. Earl F. Rebman, the president of the Salvage Committee, addressed the audience about the benefits of a Memorial Recreation Area and Driveway. Public interest was high. Twelve proposals were presented for a Memorial Boulevard along the Conestoga. But before the proposals could be brought to a vote, several people urged that further study was needed, and the vote was tabled. In the end, the city did not accept Landis' generous offer. The old Conestoga park frontage along the river was sold and is now private property.

On March 17, 1956, Robert G. Struble, who was the assistant executive director of the Brandywine Valley Association, spoke at the Millersville Men's Club meeting. After hearing a report on the work that the association was doing in the Brandywine area, Earl Rebman asked whether the Men's Club would support a similar association in Lancaster. The suggestion met with approval, and subsequently the Conestoga Valley Association was formed. The first meeting of the CVA was held at Rebman's store on April 12, 1956. Amos H. Funk was the association's first president, and Earl F. Rebman was the treasurer. The association set out upon the following statement of work:[65]

- The building of a scenic boulevard along the Conestoga, retaining the river frontage for public use from Safe Harbor to Brownstown.
- Elimination of all stream pollution.
- Reduction of soil erosion.
- Restoration of fish and wildlife.
- Improvement of woodlands.
- Preservation of wilderness areas.
- Providing recreational areas of great natural beauty.
- Preservation and restoration of historical buildings and scenic beauty sites.

On June 15, 1958, the CVA dedicated two recreational areas for public use along the Conestoga. The first was located at the confluence of the Little Conestoga Creek and the Conestoga River, and the second area was near Safe Harbor. The CVA was also instrumental in many other projects in the

Conestoga watershed. The restoration of President James Buchanan's tomb, Rock Ford, the Andrew Ellicott House, the Hans Herr House, markers for the Martin Meylin Gun shop and one for Robert Fulton were all projects made possible by the association.

EARL REBMAN

Earl Franklin Rebman was born on November 9, 1895, in Manheim Township, the son of B. Frank Rebman. His earliest jobs included working at the market and selling newspapers. He worked in the candy business and began selling and renting carnival goods. This provided the foundation to open his own store on South Queen Street. Rebman's store was well known and loved by many in the Lancaster area. He was involved in many civic organizations. He was president of the Lancaster Salvage Committee during World War II, served as president of the Lancaster Chamber of Commerce and was the founder of the Conestoga Valley Association. His book *Conestoga Watershed: Outline of History* was published in 1973. Mr. Rebman died on May 4, 1984, and is buried in the Greenwood Cemetery in Lancaster County.

HURRICANE AGNES

On June 15, 1972, near the beginning of the Atlantic hurricane season, a tropical depression formed over the Yucatan Peninsula in Mexico. The storm tracked eastward and entered the Caribbean Sea. Over the warm waters of the Caribbean, it strengthened into a tropical storm on June 16. The National Hurricane Center christened the storm Agnes. The storm gradually curved northward and passed just west of Cuba on June 17. The next day, it had increased in intensity enough to be upgraded to a hurricane. Hurricane Agnes made landfall near Panama City, Florida, on June 19. Once over land, the storm rapidly weakened and was a tropical depression again as it passed over Georgia. An article in the *Lancaster New Era* on June 20, 1972, ironically had this to say: "When you get up Wednesday morning and it's raining outside (again) and all cloudy and dreary, just go back to bed and get up Thursday morning when the effects of Hurricane Agnes should be gone and the weatherman expects clear skies." The depression strengthened to a tropical storm again while crossing North Carolina and entered the Atlantic Ocean on June 22. From there, the storm traveled up the coast and made landfall again in New York City.

Hurricane Agnes was the costliest hurricane to hit the United States at that time, causing an estimated $2.1 billion in damages with 128 deaths. The brunt of the damage, largely due to flooding, happened in Pennsylvania, especially along the Susquehanna River. In Lancaster County, Agnes dumped eight and a half inches of rain in one day. Because of the extent of the damages caused by this storm, the National Hurricane Center retired the name Agnes from its list of storm names. There will never be another Hurricane Agnes.

While most of the expensive damage caused by Hurricane Agnes was experienced by the towns along the Susquehanna River, the Conestoga also suffered in similar, albeit smaller, ways. The historic covered bridges took the brunt of the flood. Even though it is located well upstream, Kurtz's Mill covered bridge was dislodged and floated down the river. The covered bridge at Pinetown was swept away in the flood and carried downstream, where it approached the Hunsicker Mill covered bridge. Eyewitnesses reported that the Pinetown bridge floated around the Hunsicker bridge at the last moment. Minutes later, the Hunsicker bridge was also swept off its piers. Both bridges were carried farther down the river. The Pinetown bridge ended up beached along Butter Road, while the Hunsicker bridge was dashed against the piers of the abandoned trolley bridge near the iron bridge where the New Holland Pike crosses the river at Eden. At the concrete bridge carrying Route 462 at Bridgeport, the river crested several inches higher than the railings of the bridge. The steel bridge at Engleside was pushed off its piers and smashed against the nearby railroad bridge. The Conestoga River at Lancaster crested at 27.8 feet above the floodplain (normal flood stage is 11 feet). As the river rose, it also widened, reaching about fifteen to twenty times its normal width. Large quantities of Lancaster County soil in the form of fine sediment were carried down the river into the Susquehanna and eventually into the Chesapeake Bay.[66]

TRASH AND RUNOFF

All through history, people have viewed the river as a place to dispose of trash and unwanted items. The river is assumed to be an endless flow of water that washes away anything that is thrown or dumped into it. The local scuba clubs know that the best places to look for artifacts in the riverbed are under bridges and at the sites of old bridges. People had the habit of disposing of things by throwing them off the bridge as they traveled across. It is not wise to wade the Conestoga in bare feet because in some areas, the bottom is littered with broken glass. Even today, people will dump piles of trash or building supplies on the banks of the river under the assumption that they will eventually get washed away. One of the most common items seen today in and along the river are tires. Tires do not float and they do not degrade; they just sit there stuck in the mud, causing a hazard and an eyesore.

While dumping is a serious problem, not all the trash found in the river was deliberately dumped there. Much of it comes from littering or garbage spillage on the land that is later swept into the river by runoff. In the early period of the river's history, runoff was not a problem because the forest and the wetlands served as a giant sponge that slowed down the water flow

A "no littering" sign sits next to other trash picked up along the river.

The Conestoga River

A wheel and tire sit in the mud in the upper Conestoga.

enough that periods of higher precipitation could be handled with little erosive damage to the riverbanks.

When rain falls in the river valley, each raindrop will experience one of four possible fates. Some portion of the precipitation is returned to the air in the form of evaporation. Another portion is absorbed by plant life, especially trees, through the process called transpiration. Still another portion is absorbed by the soil, where it replenishes the groundwater. Any precipitation that is left over from these three processes flows into the streams and rivers as runoff. When these four processes (evaporation, transpiration, absorption and runoff) are in balance, the result is a stable ecosystem. But when the system becomes unbalanced, typically from removal of vegetation or from the construction of impervious materials, the amount of runoff increases. This, in turn, causes flash flooding to occur during periods of heavy precipitation. The flooding causes erosion and destruction of the floodplain, which serves to further exacerbate the problem.

As mentioned in the introduction, the Conestoga Valley was originally covered with forest and wetlands that served to keep the ecosystem in

A History

balance. As the trees were cleared for farming, the runoff began to increase, albeit very slowly at first. As the wetlands were drained and the water formed into stream channels, the runoff increased a little more. In the eighteenth century, the first farms were primarily focused on crops, mostly grains like wheat and flax. Livestock was mostly utilized for feeding the farm household or for transportation. The Conestoga Valley during this time was still a very wet and boggy place, making transportation difficult on rainy days. This is probably what gave rise to the commonly heard phrase in the Lancaster area, "I'll be there, Lord willin' and if the cricks don't rise."

The latter part of the eighteenth century into the nineteenth saw the beginning of the iron industry. At first, the furnaces were fired by charcoal. This required the clearing of vast acres of forest, which was usually clean cut and burned in large mounds to form the charcoal needed to keep the furnaces and forges running. The ironmasters knew that the forest was a limited resource. They practiced a form of crop rotation so that as each block of land was cleared, it was left idle to recover enough that it could be harvested again a few years later. Farmers would also cut down perhaps an acre of trees each year to supply the wood they needed for heating and cooking and then allow the trees to regrow. During the period leading up to the Civil War, the Lancaster farming community transformed from crops only to a crop-and-livestock pattern. Crops were rotated, with little land being left fallow. Livestock was raised in larger quantities to be sold at market to feed the growing city and town populations.

In the latter part of the nineteenth century, coal replaced charcoal in the iron industry. Likewise, people switched over from wood to coal as their heating source. Tobacco was introduced as the new cash crop in the agriculture industry, and farms transitioned to poultry and dairy operations. The tobacco crop did not replace the other crops that were being farmed but rather was added to them, requiring more field space. Now whenever the forest land was cleared, it was put into agricultural use. The forested area in the Conestoga Valley greatly decreased during this era. People began noticing a change in the weather patterns as the forest diminished. Rainfall became more irregular, and heavy storms accompanied by hail became more frequent. The water began running unencumbered down the hillsides, swelling the streams and causing devastating floods in the river valley.[67]

Moving into the twentieth century, dairy operations became much more common in the valley. Dairies generate manure that is used to enhance the fertility of the soil. Also in this period, artificial fertilizers and pesticides came into common use in the farming industry. These materials, both the natural and artificial kind, combined with the increased runoff into the streams and river, impacted the water quality of the Conestoga.

In 1948, a team of scientists from the Academy of Natural Sciences in Philadelphia, headed by botanist Dr. Ruth Patrick, spent the summer wading the Conestoga and its tributaries studying the plants, fish and exceptionally beautiful microscopic creatures with glass-like coatings called diatoms living in the river. Dr. Patrick developed the principle that the best way to determine the effects of man-made pollution in a stream was to study the organisms living in and near the water. Dr. Patrick's approach was to employ a team of scientists with expertise in various disciplines in biology, chemistry and physics. Her survey of the Conestoga was the first comprehensive water quality monitoring effort in North America.[68] In 1949, she published a paper titled "A Proposed Biological Measure of Stream Conditions, Based on a Survey of the Conestoga Basin, Lancaster County, Pennsylvania." Dr. Patrick was the recipient of many awards during her long career and was one of the proponents of the Clean Water Act. She served as a consultant on the board of the Pennsylvania Power and Light Company.

After the U.S. Congress enacted the Clean Water Act in 1972, the State of Pennsylvania identified priority areas in need of more study. The Conestoga River was designated a top-priority watershed. The Clean Water Act sets standards for designated uses such as drinking water supply, contact recreation (that is, swimming) and aquatic life. Minimum goals require all waterways to be "fishable" and "swimmable." As of 2004, the Conestoga River and each of its major tributaries have been listed as "impaired" according to the Clean Water Act. Sources of impairment are urban runoff, agricultural runoff, small residential runoff and groundwater. In addition, there were in 2004 more than fifty point-source nutrient dischargers in the Conestoga Watershed. The major pollutants are nitrogen and phosphorus.

Ongoing efforts to reduce the pollutant and sediment loads are focused on specific Best Management Practices (BMPs). These include streambank stabilization and fencing, riparian buffer strips, strip cropping, stormwater retention wetlands and others. For farming operations, best practices include animal waste retention, measured and timed application of manure and other fertilizers and low-till and no-till planting practices to conserve soil and reduce runoff.

A History

THE LANCASTER CONSERVANCY

The Lancaster Conservancy is a nonprofit organization dedicated to preserving and maintaining natural areas in Lancaster and York Counties. Founded in 1969 by a group of hunters, anglers and naturalists, the conservancy now manages over six thousand acres spread over forty-six nature preserves and sixty-nine conservation easements. The preserves that are nearest to the Conestoga are Holly Pointe, Windolph Landing, Conestoga Creek Nature Preserve and the Safe Harbor Nature Preserve. Except for Windolph Landing, these areas along the Conestoga are preserved for

People picking up trash during Lancaster Water Week.

natural habitat and are not intended for recreation. The conservancy hosts many public events and educational opportunities during the year. One of the largest events is Lancaster Water Week. Usually held in June each year, Water Week provides the opportunity for the community to get involved in activities that promote clean water along all of Lancaster County's waterways. On Saturday during Water Week, numerous locations along the Conestoga are designated for organized cleanup operations. People of all ages don their boots and gloves and work together to remove tons of trash and debris from the river.

Chapter 7

TWENTIETH-CENTURY STRUGGLES

ROCKY SPRINGS

In 1947, the Conestoga Traction Company ended trolley service in Lancaster County. The trolley cars were sent down to Rocky Springs, pushed off the tracks and burned (all except one, which is on display at the Manheim Historical Society).

In 1979, after years of deterioration and damage from Hurricane Agnes (1972), the park was in serious disrepair. The park was sold to Ben Brookmeyer, Mary Corthouts and Michael Ranck, who cleaned it up and attempted to open it for two years. But the park had to close due to poor attendance. Then, in 1984, an auction was held and Rocky Springs rides, memorabilia and some buildings were sold to the highest bidder. Soon after, seventeen acres of the park were sold for the River Bend Condominiums. Unfortunately, due to some blasting that occurred during the construction of the condominiums, the water in the fabled spring has slowed to a trickle. The Dentzel Carousel was sold and relocated to a theme park in Michigan and later moved to the Dollywood theme park in Tennessee, where it remained for ten years. The Wildcat coaster was torn down and burned in 1991.

"What happened to the carousel?" people want to know. In the late 1990s, the Rocky Springs Carousel Association was formed. It purchased the carousel and brought it home to Lancaster. Since 2005, fifteen of the forty-eight carved animals have been restored. The last mention of the project that the author

The Conestoga River

The Carousel house at Rocky Springs.

could find was published by Lancaster Newspapers in 2011, and several possible locations for the carousel to be placed were mentioned. The locations suggested were Clipper Stadium, Lancaster Square, the Lancaster Convention Center or Long's Park. However, a carousel cannot be successful as a primary attraction. The best location would be one that already has a successful entertainment business. So, none of the above locations were deemed suitable. The cost to build an enclosure and install the carousel would be measured in millions of dollars. But a suitable location and a business plan must be in place before funding can be sought. So, we wait. But it appears very unlikely that the carousel will return to Rocky Springs Park.

ROCKY SPRINGS SATURDAY NIGHT

Lyrics by Bobbi Carmitchell

There is a place I remember, down by the outskirts of town
It's hidden by time under brambles and vines and most of it's all fallen down.
Oh, when I was a kid I remember as the bus broke the crest of the hill

A History

You could still see the shell of the old roller coaster and I tried to imagine the thrill.
When the music would drift down the water and the band played well into the night,
The Jack Rabbit's running and young hearts are becoming intwined underneath the pale moonlit night.
An oh, how I wish I could be there, the calliope shiny and bright.
The carousel spinnin', the good guys are winnin', a Rocky Springs Saturday Night.

SUNNYSIDE

The Conestoga flows southward as it approaches Rocky Springs and then makes a sharp turn and flows northward again past the site of the old city water works. Then, as the river approaches the hill on which rests the County Home, it bends to the south again and heads down toward Indian Rock and Rock Ford. The 129-acre peninsula that the river so forms is known by the locals as Sunnyside. The northern third of the peninsula had been devoted to farmland for the County Home but today is the location of the Lancaster County Youth Intervention Center. The former Brenner Quarry operation dominated the center third, now filled with water, while the lower third is residential.

Local legend has it that Sunnyside began in the early twentieth century as a place for wealthy city dwellers to build summer homes to escape the heat of the city. Collective memory may have embellished the truth a bit, or perhaps it was a difference in perspective. On August 29, 1912, New Jersey developers Frank H.H. Boody and James K. O'Dea purchased forty-three acres in the southern section of the Sunnyside Peninsula from the estate of Lancaster physician Samuel T. Davis.[69] They subdivided the property into 531 lots, each twenty feet wide with varying depths. The lots were advertised for sale in 1912 for between twenty-nine and seventy-nine dollars with easy terms: five dollars down and fifty cents per week. The buyers in the next few years were predominantly working-class people. The original dwellings were owner-built structures, with a few of them being mail-order homes from Sears or other suppliers. The road network that the developers laid out was unsuitable for the topography of the area, making it impossible to fully construct the roads as designed. On top of that, there was no running water and no sewer facilities on the peninsula.

The Conestoga River

Whether or not Sunnyside started out as a rustic resort for middle-class residents, by 1933, the area was identified by the Home Owners' Loan Corporation as a distressed area, and the HOLC redlined the area, making it difficult if not impossible for the owners to secure loans for improving their properties. The houses were described by visiting officials as "shacks" and the residents as "low-paid workers." Even though the peninsula technically belonged to West Lampeter Township, both the 1929 Nolan Plan and the 1945 Baker Plan included Sunnyside in the recommendations for city improvement. Both plans advocated reserving the land along the river for use as parkland and envisioned a time when "the Lancaster region will have a parkway along the Conestoga Creek reaching to the Susquehanna River." Nothing was done, at least in Sunnyside, to implement any of the planners' recommendations.

By 1950, most of the houses were in serious disrepair, and the residents received little in services from the township. The old Conestoga Traction Company trolley line to Rocky Springs, which passed through the peninsula, had been discontinued. A farmer from Willow Street, Raymond Grimm, acquired rights to the trolley right-of-way and moved eight railroad boxcars onto the property. Grimm claimed that the cars were to be used for storing hog feed, but after adding doors, windows and room dividers, he began renting them for about twenty dollars a month. The Sunnyside residents objected strongly to this development and filed a lawsuit, but in the end, the township approved the use of the boxcars as residences largely because there was no zoning ordinance at the time. Oddly enough, the Lancaster County commissioners also approved this use of the boxcars.

Then on March 16, 1954, a fire engulfed one of the cars and a two-year-old girl, Reba K. Waltman, perished. This generated another public outcry over the boxcars. A newspaper reporter noted that the pumps that were to provide water for the area were contaminated, forcing residents to walk a quarter mile to the spring at Williamson Park to get their drinking water. The only latrines were some rough toilets with the dirt scooped out under them. Even after this, nothing was done to improve the situation.

In 1955, many of the Sunnyside residents pressed the city to take ownership of the peninsula in the hopes that a larger entity would be able to provide better services. In September of that year, Sunnyside was annexed to Lancaster City. Mayor Kendig C. Bare assured the residents that city services would be extended to Sunnyside as soon as was economically feasible. Now they would have fire and police support, as well as emergency repairs to roadways. The mayor also announced that the city would

A History

eliminate substandard housing, beginning with Grimm's boxcars. Water and sewer still proved to be a challenge, however, due to the rocky terrain. The following year, the boxcars were vacated but not removed. Other houses were condemned, but none were demolished.

In 1960, the City Planning Commission performed a study to assess the situation and needs on the Sunnyside Peninsula. The study found that approximately 450 persons lived there, predominantly white. Of the 135 dwellings, 95 percent were substandard, lacking water, sewer and adequate heating and ventilation. However, the commission also determined that the cost to bring water, sewer and lighting to the neighborhood and to repair the streets would be prohibitively expensive. The tax assessments of the properties there would never be able to pay the costs. The commission concluded that the only remedy that could succeed would be to clear all existing structures and start over. This confirmed to the residents that what they suspected was true—the city had no concern for them and had no desire to spend the money to improve their neighborhood. As the city turned its focus on other, more promising urban renewal projects, Sunnyside remained on the back burner.

In July 1968, the spring at Williamson Park, where Sunnyside residents would draw their water, became polluted due to a landfill on the hill above Indian Rock. Residents attended the July city council meeting to once again urge the city to resolve their water needs. An outbreak of hepatitis made the need imperative. The city authorized that a water line be constructed to bring water to the peninsula. But at the same time, the city designated Sunnyside as its number-one priority in the Community Renewal Plan. This was interpreted to mean complete demolition of the properties on the peninsula and relocation of its residents to public housing elsewhere in the city. In 1969, the city extended a water line onto the peninsula and built a central water house for use of all residents. At the same time, the city enacted a more stringent housing code, forcing owners to demolish condemned and vacant properties. The Grimm boxcars were finally removed.

By 1971, there were still no clear plans on how to handle the situation at Sunnyside. By this time, perhaps due to their isolation and common struggles, the Sunnyside residents had developed a strong sense of community and loyalty to the place and their neighbors. Yet another planning firm, a Philadelphia firm known as FRIDAY, made a study of the peninsula and was strongly impressed by that sense of community. The firm identified two major issues to be resolved: a large automobile junkyard and a rapidly expanding quarry operation that was threatening to consume a large portion of the real estate. While the FRIDAY plan called for the replacement of almost every structure in Sunnyside, it planned to accomplish that with as little dislocation of the residents as possible. According to this plan, Sunnyside would remain a community for low- and middle-income families. The plan also called for a walking and biking trail along the Conestoga and several bridges to provide better access to the peninsula. Once again, the cost of implementing such a plan proved to be more than the city could afford to tackle.

Then, in 1972, Hurricane Agnes struck, causing tremendous flooding damage in the state and all along the Conestoga River. Many properties located on or near the floodplain were severely damaged to the point that they needed to be demolished. While Pennsylvania received funding to recover from the storm, Sunnyside was once again overlooked. By 1980, Sunnyside's population had dwindled to around 175, many of them with incomes below the poverty line. Finally, in 1984, several Sunnyside residents attended a public hearing to set priorities for the allocation of Community Development Block Grant funds. The residents argued that the city needed to assume the cost of installing water and sewer lines in the community. Mayor Arthur Morris agreed, and two months later, the mayor announced that CDBG funds had been set aside to begin a multiyear project to bring water and sewer service to Sunnyside. Construction of the water and sewer lines along with improvements to the roads necessitated the demolition of a few more residences. Habitat for Humanity built a new house for one of the residents, and the city assisted the others with finding new homes. The water/sewer project was completed in 1989, finally giving the residents services that they had been wanting for decades. The auto junkyard has been cleaned up, the quarry operation ended and the quarry was filled with water. The county built a Youth Intervention Center on the north end of the peninsula in 2001. But as property values improved, some landlords saw the opportunity to raise rents, making it difficult for some residents to remain in their homes. Once again, the future of Sunnyside remains clouded.

PUBLIC SWIMMING

As the population increased and the river became increasingly polluted, the prospect of swimming in the river became less desirable and less healthy. As a result, swimming pools opened around the county that provided safe, clean locations for the public to cool off during the hot summer months. Brookside pool opened in 1914, the Crystal Pool at Rocky Springs opened in 1921 and a third pool at Maple Grove Park opened around this time as well. While these three pools were promoted as public pools, they did not admit African Americans. The situation did not change even after the Equal Rights Act of 1939 mandated that public facilities could not discriminate by race. Most persons of color during this time were obliged to swim in a designated place in the dirty Conestoga known as the "pogie."

In 1960, a group of activists set out to demonstrate that the county pools were posing as membership clubs as a tactic for excluding African Americans. They visited Maple Grove, Brookside and Rocky Springs and organized test cases called "sandwiches" where a white person applied for membership, followed by a black person, followed by another white person. In every case, the first white applicant paid the fee and was immediately admitted to the pool. The black person was asked to fill out an application form and told they would have to wait several weeks to find out whether they would be admitted. After the black person was denied, the second white swimmer came up to the desk, paid the fee and was immediately admitted.

Using these test cases as evidence, three civil rights cases were opened against the three county pools. Robert Pfannebecker litigated all three cases for the plaintiffs. As the cases slowly made their way through the courts, people got impatient for action to be taken. In the summer of 1963, a protest march was organized at Rocky Springs to push for integration. Eventually, the courts ruled in favor of the plaintiffs and upheld the requirement that public facilities must be open to all. The result was that all three pools changed their status from "open access" to "members only" to sidestep the state civil rights law. A reason given by at least one of the pools was the fear that if they opened their membership to blacks, the white members would all leave, and the pool would no longer be economically viable.

In response to this situation, Lancaster City built the Conestoga Pines pool with taxpayer money. Conestoga Pines opened in 1966 as the first integrated pool in Lancaster County. The county followed suit by building the Central Park pool in 1967. Other cities around the country opened pools in African American neighborhoods, but they tended to be small, aboveground pools with few amenities. The county pool, by contrast, was a modern, high-quality pool hailed as "the best pool in the county." Conestoga Pines and the Central Park pools remain open today to serve all Lancastrians.

Chapter 8
PARKS AND RECREATION

The previous chapters outline some of the negative aspects that human activity imposes on the Conestoga watershed. But the Conestoga does provide a growing list of places that have been reserved for recreational activity. Some of these areas are private, but many of them are open to the public. This chapter lists the various parks and recreation areas along the Conestoga River. This is not intended to be a comprehensive list. New areas may have opened and others may have closed by the time you read this, so please check the status of any of the sites on this list before you plan to visit them. These are listed in order as the river flows.

HISTORIC POOLE FORGE

Poole Forge is the site of a colonial iron forge. The grounds include the iron master's mansion, the paymaster's building, two tenant houses, a covered bridge and a limekiln. The grounds are well kept and are a great place for a family picnic or just a quiet place to relax. There is also a pavilion that may be rented for picnics or reunions. The paymaster's house operates as a bed-and-breakfast if you wish to stay the night. The mansion and grounds are available for rentals and are a popular wedding spot. Poole Forge is located just west of Churchtown on PA Route 23 at Poole Forge Road.

People wading in the river at Poole Forge.

CONESTOGA VALLEY CAMP ASSOCIATION

This is a private, members-only camp located along Turtle Hill Road.

WEST EARL COMMUNITY PARK

The West Earl Community Park is located along PA Route 772 between Talmage and Brownstown. This park was built by the West Earl Lions Club and is now managed by the township. The park has a pavilion that may be rented, a children's playground, a large open space and two walking trails that offer a beautiful stroll along the Conestoga River. If you look carefully, you will find the piers for the old Conestoga Traction Company trolley line hidden in the trees along the river.

SILVAN B. FISHER TOWNSHIP PARK

On the other side of Route 772, across from the West Earl Park, is the Silvan B. Fisher Township Park (aka Stone Quarry Park). This park is managed by West Earl Township and offers two walking trails and small boat access to the Conestoga River. The park is named in honor of Silvan B. Fisher, who served many years as the township roadmaster, supervisor and firefighter.

521 CLUB

Located along Butter Road with frontage on the river is the 521 Club. This is a meeting place for recovering alcoholics. Various meetings and events for Alcoholics Anonymous are held here. Access is for members only.

PERELMAN PARK

Perelman Park is located on Paper Mill Road off Landis Valley Road near the site of Binkley's Bridge and the Printer's Paper Mill. Perelman Park is a five-acre park managed by Manheim Township that offers a nature trail, butterfly garden and canoe access to the river.

LANCASTER COUNTRY CLUB

Lancaster Country Club is a private country club located along the New Holland Pike. The club features a golf course that spans both sides of the Conestoga River. LCC hosted the U.S. Women's Open in 2015.

CONESTOGA PINES

Accessed from Pitney Road east of Lancaster, the Conestoga Pines park includes a public swimming pool, open spaces, picnic tables and boat access

A History

Kayakers at Perelman Park.

to the river. Opened in 1966, Conestoga Pines was the first integrated pool in Lancaster County.

WATERWORKS DAM CANOE ACCESS

There is a canoe access point just below the dam at the Lancaster pumping station. There is also an exit point just above the dam for portage around the dam.

GROFFTOWN ROAD

Lancaster Township manages a small park with walking trails along the old Grofftown Road along the river below the Conestoga Viaduct. Access is from Ranck Mill Road/Conestoga Drive and Grofftown Road. This section of walkways will eventually be part of the Greater Lancaster Heritage Pathway, which is planned to provide a walking and biking route between Lancaster and Leola.

ROCKY SPRINGS BED-AND-BREAKFAST

In 2001, Rocky Springs was bought by Sam and Elaine Stoltzfus, who restored the mansion house and opened it as a bed-and-breakfast. Rocky Springs today is a quiet refuge. The Rock Springs B&B offers four rooms in the mansion house and a separate cottage in a quiet area with frontage on the Conestoga. Rocky Springs B&B is located along Millport Road next to the Rocky Springs bowling alley.

HOLLY POINTE PARK AND NATURE PRESERVE

Holly Pointe Nature Preserve is one of the Lancaster Conservancy preserves. It is located at the end of Holly Lane on the peninsula around the corner from the old location of People's Bathing Resort. There is a small playground on Holly Lane. The preserve is being managed for habitat. A trail is not maintained.

CONESTOGA GREENWAY TRAIL

The Conestoga Greenway Trail runs along the Conestoga River across from the Sunnyside Peninsula from South Conestoga Drive to South Duke Street. Parking is available on South Conestoga Drive near Betz Road, on South Broad Street and at the trail's end on South Duke Street. A short walk across the Duke Street bridge leads to access to the Lancaster County Park.

The Lancaster Inter-Municipal Committee (LIMC), a group of municipalities in central Lancaster County that cooperate on selected local government activities, completed the Conestoga Greenway Plan in 1999. The purpose of the plan is to provide for active and passive recreation, education and environmental preservation along the Conestoga. The trail is a prototype for a greenway along the rest of the waterway.

A History

The bed-and-breakfast at Rocky Springs.

Holly Pointe Park.

Conestoga Greenway Trail.

WILLIAMSON PARK

Williamson Park is named after the land donor, department store owner H.S. Williamson, who donated the plot to the city in 1897. The park included the Edward Hand mansion, Indian Rock, the Horseshoe Spring and the old ford across the Conestoga. Not much was done to improve the park until approximately 1907, when Lancaster mayor J.P. McCaskey appointed Albert Goodwin to be the park officer. Goodwin started a nursery to grow trees for the park and created flower beds and walkways with benches. By 1910, the park was considered one of Lancaster's most beautiful assets. The entrance to Williamson Park is on the east side of the Conestoga at the entrance of the Sunnyside Peninsula. A path led from there to the Rocky Springs trolley line. Today, the park is adjacent to, and considered part of, the Lancaster County Central Park. The old ford is gone, and unfortunately, the Horseshoe Spring had to be closed because seepage from a landfill above Indian Rock contaminated the water. There is a persistent legend that Indian Rock is so named because an Indian maiden jumped off the cliff to her death. However, stories similar to that one are attached to many cliffs and waterfalls around the country. From the legend of Winona in Wisconsin, to the Maid of the Mists at Niagara, to Multnomah Falls in

A History

The view from Indian Rock in Williamson Park.

Oregon, it must have been common practice for Indian maidens to jump off cliffs. It is very doubtful that the Conestoga version is anything more than folklore. Another interesting note is that there is a Williamson Park in Lancaster, England, but that park apparently has no relationship to the one in Lancaster, Pennsylvania.

ROCK FORD

Rock Ford is the eighteenth-century home of Revolutionary War general Edward Hand. In the 1950s, after centuries of neglect, it was owned by the Lancaster Area Refuse Authority and was slated to be demolished to make room for an incinerator and landfill. The Junior League of Lancaster purchased the house and adjacent grounds in 1957, and the Rock Ford Foundation was established in 1958 to restore and maintain the grounds. The house opened to the public in 1960. Today, Rock Ford offers many tours and educational opportunities to learn about life in the eighteenth century, not just for the white landowners but also the slaves and others who contributed to the plantation's success.

The Conestoga River

LANCASTER COUNTY CENTRAL PARK

Lancaster County Central Park is 544 acres of land bordering the Conestoga River just south of Lancaster City. In May 1955, 439 acres were annexed to the city, including the older Williamson Park and Kiwanis Park and lands that were part of the Ira H. Landis estate. The swimming pool opened on Memorial Day 1967. The park offers many facilities, including a public swimming pool, pavilions, a beautifully landscaped Garden of Five Senses, public garden plots, camping and many hiking trails. In addition, there is about two miles of frontage along the river.

MEADIA HEIGHTS GOLF CLUB

Founded in 1922, the Meadia Heights Golf Club is a private golf club located on the south side of the river below Lancaster City.

D.F. BUCHMILLER COUNTY PARK

Buchmiller Park was made possible by a bequeath of the estate of Dulon F. Buchmiller, who was the founder of the Safe Padlock and Hardware Company. The money was used to buy a farm and set up the park in 1925. Fulton National Bank manages the trust fund that maintains the park.

WINDOLPH LANDING NATURE PRESERVE

The Windolph Landing Nature Preserve consists of twenty-two acres of land set aside by the Lancaster Conservancy along a bend in the river south of Lancaster's west end. Access to the preserve is from the Second Lock Road. Windolph Landing has a unique environment where groundwater seeps down a steep hillside of limestone bedrock that leads into the Conestoga. A marked trail loops from the parking area down to the river and back.

A History

The Garden of Five Senses in Lancaster County Central Park.

Windolph Landing Nature Preserve.

WINDOLPH LANDING PARK

Windolph Landing Park offers open space along the riverfront with a children's playground, picnic tables, a pavilion and a hiking trail. The park is at the bottom of the Windolph Landing housing development on Wilderness Road that may be accessed from Bean Road.

CIRCLE M CAMPING RESORT

The Circle M RV and Camping Resort sits inside a loop of the river just east of the Borough of Millersville. Circle M offers nearly three hundred camping sites, indoor and outdoor swimming pools, tennis courts and many other resort amenities.

ROCK HILL ACCESS AREA

Operated by the Pennsylvania Fish Commission, the Rock Hill Access area is located on Long Lane at the north end of the Conestoga Boulevard. Rock Hill provides off-street parking for boating access for fishing and canoeing.

CONESTOGA RIVER PARK

The Conestoga River Park is located along the Conestoga Boulevard just north of River Road. This park was formed from lands reserved by the Conestoga Valley Association. The park has picnic tables and green space and features one of the surviving locks built by the Conestoga Navigation Company.

SAFE HARBOR PARK

Safe Harbor Park is located along River Road in Safe Harbor. The park is maintained by Brookfield Renewable, the company that operates the Safe

Conestoga River Park near Safe Harbor.

Harbor hydroelectric plant. The park includes tennis courts, a ball diamond and a small pavilion that may be rented.

LOW-GRADE RAIL TRAIL

The Enola Low-Grade Rail Trail follows the old Enola rail line from Turkey Hill to Safe Harbor. One of the trail heads is located along Powerhouse Road near the point where the Conestoga enters the Susquehanna River.

CONESTOGA RIVER WATER TRAIL

The Conestoga River is a Class 1 river, making it a popular waterway for canoes and kayaks. Table 3 provides a list of locations providing boat access to the river. Access locations change frequently, so please check on their availability before using them. Also, all boaters are expected to observe the "leave no trace" rule of Pennsylvania boating.

CONESTOGA RIVER CLUB

The Conestoga River Club was formed in 2020 by boating enthusiasts. It is focused on improving and maintaining public access points along the Conestoga River Trail. The hope is to extend the trail to the full length of the river.

TABLE 3: BOAT ACCESS POINTS

Location	Coordinates
Sylvan B. Fisher Park	40.120637, -76.213877
Perelman Park	40.0827999, -76.2602234
Conestoga Pines Park	40.0532418, -76.2727547
Conestoga Drive North	40.0450947, -76.2742996
Conestoga Greenway	40.0358951, -76.2796211
Rock Ford Road	40.0231451, -76.2888908
Lancaster County Park	40.0231451, -76.2888908
Windolph Landing Park	40.0025034, -76.3235664
Creek Drive North	40.001057, -76.3439941
Creek Drive South	39.9985585, -76.3450241
Slackwater	39.9856699, -76.3566113
Rock Hill	39.9629118, -76.3656235
Conestoga River Park	39.9364608, -76.3865662
Safe Harbor Park	39.9317552, -76.3841629
Safe Harbor Park	39.9298136, -76.3830471

TABLE 4: DAMS

Location	Coordinates
Farm	40.140028, -75.994074
Spring Grove Mill	40.143887, -76.020086
Along Rt. 625	40.140398, -76.029602

Location	Coordinates
Linden Road	40.139978, -76.048147
White Oak Ice	40.145665, -76.077290
Crooked Lane	40.139920, -76.167783
Mill Road	40.150103, -76.092884
Kurtz Road	40.150844, -76.103670
Cider Mill Road	40.141205, -76.150614
Bushong's Mill	40.104570, -76.237670
Water Plant	40.051204, -76.276362
Conestoga Viaduct	40.050046, -76.278005

THE CONESTOGA BOULEVARD (PROPOSAL FOR THE FUTURE)

The 1929 Nolan Plan and the 1945 Baker Plan both advocated for a greenway "boulevard" along the Conestoga River. Earl Rebman and the Conestoga Valley Association proposed a greenway from Brownstown to Safe Harbor. Many opportunities have been lost since those efforts, but the current Conestoga Greenway trail is a start. That trail begins near the site of the old city mill and follows the curve of the river, ending at South Duke Street. From there, it is possible to cross the bridge and enter Williamson Park. The county park borders the river all the way beyond the location of Riegart's Landing, the old head of navigation for the Conestoga Navigation Company.

The author would like to propose that the Conestoga Greenway trail be extended to follow the old towpath from Riegart's Landing (now Strawberry Street) all the way to the Conestoga River Park at Safe Harbor. We would need to find a way to connect the county park with Buchmiller Park on the other side of the Willow Street Pike. From there, the trail could follow the old Quarryville Railroad bed down past the first lock as far as the Mill Stream. I am sure there would be many challenges to such a project, but what a way for people to enjoy the beautiful asset to our county that is the Conestoga River.

What will happen next has not been written yet. The decisions and actions we take today will affect the stories that follow. It is good to look at the past

The Conestoga River

to understand how we got to where we are today and to, hopefully, learn from mistakes that were made in the past. We do not want to be too critical of the people who came before us. They were acting on the knowledge and goals that they had at the time. But we can look at our current practices with a critical eye to ensure that we are making the best use of the resources that we have and with an eye to the future so that our children and grandchildren will be able to enjoy these resources in the same or, perhaps, better condition than we inherited them.

> *Life—like the Summer leaves,*
> *Fade once forever!*
> *Life-like this gliding stream*
> *Flows backward never?*
> *On to the silent sea,*
> *On to eternity,*
> *Thus sing thy waves to me,*
> *O Conestoga.*
> —author unknown

Appendix A

TIMELINE

1608: Susquehannocks are in Indian Town Manor Township.
1658: Josiah Cole and a band of Quakers meet with the Susquehannocks at their village.
March 4, 1681: Pennsylvania charter signed by King Charles II to William Penn.
1684: Penn returns to England.
1699: Penn returns to Pennsylvania with James Logan.
1700: Conestogoes (remnant of Susquehannocks) are located at Turkey Hill.
1706: A group of Quakers visit Conestoga Indian town. "Queen" Conguegas is consulted on the possibility of holding a religious service.
1711: First Mennonites settle in the county.
1715: Scotch-Irish settle in Lancaster County.
July 8, 1717: Governor William Keith holds a conference with the Shawnee at Conestoga.
1717–18: Conestoga Manor surveyed by Jacob Taylor.
1718: William Penn dies after suffering the effects of a stroke for several years.
1718: Conestogoe Township is formed.
1719: Hans Herr House is built.
1720: James Login holds conference at Conestoga.
1720: West Conestoga Township is formed (later called Donegal).
1725: Postlethwait's tavern is mentioned on Conestoga Creek near Rockville.
1728: Stephen Atkinson builds the first mill on the Conestoga, a fulling mill between Reigart's and Graeff's Landings.
May 10, 1729: Lancaster County is formed.

Appendix A

1730: King's Highway opens.

1730: Town of Lancaster is laid out by James Hamilton.

January 3, 1733: David Jenkins applies for a grant of four hundred acres along the Conestoga River below Morgantown.

December 3, 1739: Michael Baughman asks to purchase Indian Town in an effort to remove the Indians from Conestogoe Manor.

1740: Thomas Morgan builds a small stone chapel near the confluence of the East and West Branches.

1742: Lancaster organizes as a borough.

1742: William Bronson builds a forge and mansion (later called Windsor Forge Mansion, aka Windsor Place).

1754: French and Indian War starts.

1760: William Henry (rifle maker) visits England, returns and builds a steam paddleboat on the Conestoga.

1763: Pontiac war.

December 14, 1763: "Paxtang Boys" surround Indian Town, kill and scalp six of the Conestogas and burn the buildings.

December 27, 1763: Massacre at Lancaster workhouse.

circa 1768: First bridge is built over the Conestoga at Hinkletown.

March 7, 1776: Edward Hand is given command of the Pennsylvania Regiment.

September 24, 1777: Continental Congress comes to Lancaster.

1777: Robert Fulton (then fourteen) visits William Henry to study his steamboat.

1779: Poole Forge is built by James Olds (the father of Ann (Olds) Coleman).

1779: Robert Fulton experiments with paddle wheels on the Conestoga.

1779: Christian Binkley (1738–1805) builds a mill on the Conestoga.

1785: Rock Ford mansion is built.

1789: Spring Grove Forge mansion is built.

1789: Binkley's Covered Bridge is built near Eden.

1792: Construction begins on the Philadelphia and Lancaster Turnpike (finished in 1794).

1792: George Graeff's tavern is built at Engleside.

1796: Witmer's first bridge (wooden).

1799: Witmer's stone arch bridge is built.

1806: Henry Slaymaker builds a stone arch bridge at Graeff's Tavern.

May 15, 1824: Petition to make the Conestoga navigable.

January 1829: Conestoga Navigation Company begins service.

circa 1829: Wooden railroad bridge is built over Conestoga.

Appendix A

1834–87: Henry Leman Long Rifle forge at Pinetown.
1836: Lancaster's first pumping station is built.
February 22, 1837: Water is introduced to Lancaster City.
April 1, 1837: Coleman founds Lancaster, Susquehanna and Slackwater Navigation Company.
1838: Susquehanna and Tidewater Canal opens.
1844: Steamer *Conestoga* begins trips between Philadelphia and Lancaster.
1846: Safe Harbor Furnace begins operation.
1846: Conestoga Cotton Mills begins operation.
August 1848: Safe Harbor Rolling Mill, Safe Harbor Iron Works begin operation.
1855: Wabank House completed.
1855: Rocky Springs Hotel is built.
1856: Brownstown Mill begins operation.
1859: Poole Forge covered bridge is built.
1866: Final sheriff's sale of Conestoga Navigation.
1866: Shober's Paper Mill at Slackwater begins operation.
1866: Printer's Paper Mill established at Binkley's Bridge.
1867: Old Binkley's Bridge collapses.
1868: Replacement for Binkley's Bridge is begun (finished 1869).
1868: Spring Grove Mill is built.
1878: Weaver's Mill covered bridge is built.
1878: Steam pumps added to Lancaster Water Plant.
1882: Demuth Park opens (Rocky Springs).
1882: Binkley's second bridge and papermill are burned.
1886: Coal-fired electrical generation at Engleside.
1887–88: Conestoga Creek Viaduct is built.
1888: Second Lancaster water pumping station is built.
1890: John Peoples leases Rocky Springs.
July 4, 1890: Launching of the *Lady Gay*.
August 10, 1895: Conestoga Boulevard is opened.
1896: Griffiths and Weiner lease Rocky Springs.
1896: *Emma Belle* and *Evelyn B.* steamboats are built.
1897: Slackwater dam converted to generate electric power, also Rock Hill.
1898: Iron Bridge (on Iron Bridge Road) is built.
1899: Rocky Springs is bought by Thomas Rees.
1900: Lancaster Country Club is established in Rossmere.
1901: Wabank Electric Power Plant is built.
1903: Levan's Mill is destroyed by fire.

Appendix A

May 5, 1903: Williamson Park is formed.
May 10, 1903: Trolley service begins to Rocky Springs.
March 8, 1904: Safe Harbor destroyed by ice flood.
January 5, 1912: Frank Diffenderfer's plea for the Conestoga River.
September 20, 1912: A commemoration of Lancaster County in the Revolution is held at Indian Rock in Williamson Park.
1913: Buchanan Water & Power Company is chartered at Wabank, Lancaster County P&W at Slackwater, Hamilton W&P at Rock Hill and Stevens W&P at Rock Hill.
1913: Lancaster Country Club is moved to its present location.
1915: *Lady Gay*'s last trip.
1918: Jack Rabbit is built at Rocky Springs.
March 1922: The last remnant of People's Resort, the roller rink, is torn down. Sewage water in the creek made the water unfit for bathing. Bathhouses are destroyed by fire.
1923: Iron truss bridge at Rock Hill is built.
1924: Rocky Springs Carousel.
1928: Wildcat is built.
1929: Nolan Plan recommends scenic boulevard and wider bridge over Conestoga.
February 1931: Lancaster Chamber article: "Scenic Beauty or Open Sewer?"
1933: Witmer's Bridge is demolished and replaced with new concrete bridge.
1945–46: Baker Plan urges a scenic drive and open spaces.
1946: Earl Rebman is named president of Lancaster Chamber.
July 20, 1946: Ira H. Landis offers the city 1.5 miles of river frontage.
1947: End of Trolley service.
June 15, 1948: Biological study of the Conestoga watershed begun by Dr. Ruth Patrick of the Philadelphia Academy of Natural Sciences.
1951: Soil conservation program set up countywide.
1954: Joe Figari buys Rocky Springs.
March 17, 1956: Conestoga Valley Association (CVA) formed.
July 11, 1956: CVA decides to build a scenic boulevard retaining river frontage for public use from Safe Harbor to Brownstown.
May 8, 1958: Lancaster City and county medical group approve adequate sewage disposal for metropolitan area.
June 15, 1958: CVA dedicates two recreational areas, one at the confluence of Little Conestoga and the other at Safe Harbor.
February 20, 1960: Train wreck on Conestoga Viaduct.

Appendix A

1961: Project 70, a seven-year, $7 million plan by PA State Planning Board, is announced to expand state parks and recreation.
July 1, 1961: U.S. Geological staff begin two-year study of water resources in Conestoga watershed. Annual sediment load is eighty-four thousand tons.
February 28, 1962: Earl Rebman unveils new Conestoga Boulevard map.
1965: Rocky Springs closes.
1965: Proposal for creation of Lancaster County Park.
March 1965: Lancaster Area Sewer Authority is formed.
August 1966: Survey is done to assess future water needs of the county.
1968: Second lock bridge destroyed by vandals.
1969: Lancaster County Park is created.
1969: Lancaster Conservancy is formed.
June 13, 1969: Ad in *Lancaster New Era*: "Now is the time to set aside land for a Parkway."
June 1972: Hurricane Agnes hits.
1972: Construction begins of Washington Boro sewage treatment plant.
1977: Clean Water Act instituted by U.S. Congress.
1979: Conestoga Headwaters Rural Clean Water Program is implemented.
1982: USGS begins water quality study of Conestoga headwaters.
2001: Rocky Springs Bed-and-Breakfast opens.
July 2015: Women's U.S. Open at Lancaster Country Club.

Appendix B

BRIDGES

Location	Township	Coordinates
Limekiln Road	Caernarvon Township	40.149219, -75880842
Twin County Road (Route 10)	Caernarvon Township	40.140182, -75.903523
S. Red School Road	Caernarvon Township	40.138975, -75.913793
Maxwell Hill Road	Caernarvon Township	40.136718, -75.922066
Farm Lane	Caernarvon Township	40.134792, -75930941
Shirktown Road	Caernarvon Township	40.133003, -75.936456
Boot Jack Road	Caernarvon Township	40.129598, -75.956169
Farm Lane	Caernarvon Township	40.127411, -75.960072
S. Churchtown Road	Caernarvon Township	40.128254, -75.965079
Poole Forge Covered Bridge	Caernarvon Township	40.129867, -75.976398
Route 23	Caernarvon Township	40.131679, -75.977471
Farm Bridge	Caernarvon Township	40.134514, -75.980688
Mill Road	Caernarvon Township	40.136711, -75.993444
Weaver's Mill Covered Bridge	East Earl Township	40.141112, -75.998027

Appendix B

Location	Township	Coordinates
Iron Bridge Road	East Earl Township	40.144727, -76.010222
Spring Grove Forge	East Earl Township	40.143841, -75.020683
Reading Road (PA 625)	East Earl Township	40.141967, -76.031539
Conestoga Creek Road	East Earl Township	40.140434, -76.041068
Weaverland Valley Road (PA 897)	East Earl Township	40.138933, -76.046425
Linden Road	East Earl Township	40.139978, -75.048147
Weaverland Bridge	East Earl Township	40.137787, -76.059519
White Oak Road	East Earl Township	40.145720, -76.077796
Gristmill Road	East Earl Township	40.149522, -76.090380
Kurtz's Mill	East Earl Township	40.150700, -76.103844
Hinkletown (U.S. 322)	East Earl Township	40.153341, -76.127866
Footbridge	East Earl Township	40.150206, -76.138387
Bitzer's Mill Covered Bridge	East Earl Township	40.140397, -76.151959
North Farmersville Road	East Earl Township	40.134848, -76.174125
Brownstown Mill Bridge	West Earl Township	40.127922, -76.199655
Private driveway	West Earl Township	40.118507, -76.207986
Talmage (PA 772)	West Earl Township	40.120509, -76.213662
Bushong's Mill	Upper Leacock Township	40.105229, -76.237820
Pinetown Covered Bridge	Upper Leacock Township	40.105646, -76.248198
Hunsecker's Mill Covered Bridge	Upper Leacock Township	40.087427, -76.247843
New Holland Pike (PA 23)	Upper Leacock Township	40.077553, -76.259309
Umble's Mill Bridge	Upper Leacock Township	40.070957, -76.262697

Appendix B

Location	Township	Coordinates
Golf cart path	Upper Leacock Township	40.061680, -76.266793
Golf cart path	Upper Leacock Township	40.060220, -76.268106
U.S. Route 30	Upper Leacock Township	40.057827, -76.273041
East Walnut Street (PA 23)	Upper Leacock Township	40.053550, -76.272119
Water Plant Bridge	Upper Leacock Township	40.051204, -76.276362
Conestoga Creek Viaduct	East Lampeter Township	40.050016, -76.277936
Lincoln Highway (PA 462)	East Lampeter Township	40.037807, -76.273339
Circle Avenue	Lancaster Township	40.032667, -76.286921
Sunnyside	Lancaster Township	40.023664, -76.283898
Riegart's Landing	Lancaster Township	40.028349, -76.297563
U.S. 222/PA 272 North	Lancaster Township	40.021189, -76.302577
Engleside	Lancaster Township	40.021605, -76.304203
New Danville Pike (PA 324)	Lancaster Township	39.996895, -76.311259
Millersville Road (PA 741)	Lancaster Township	40.000872, -76.328041
Stehman Road	Conestoga Township	39.983926, -76.357070
Rock Hill	Conestoga Township	39.961592, -76.365638
Safe Harbor	Conestoga Township	39.939082, -76.387381
Powerhouse Road	Conestoga Township	39.925806, -76.384317
Safe Harbor Trestle	Conestoga Township	39.925638, -76.384306
Port Road Bridge	Conestoga Township	39.925231, -76.384390

Appendix C

MILLS

Common Name	Township	Disposition	Built	Coordinates
Spring Mill (Zug's)	Caernarvon	Business	1823	40.138193, -75.912417
Fairview Roller Mill	Caernarvon	Site	1816	40.133981, -75.931600
Upper Windsor Gristmill	Caernarvon	Site	1860	40.129602, -75.956582
Windsor Mill	Caernarvon	Farm	1863	40.128097, -75.956679
Pool Forge Gristmill	Caernarvon	Site	1733	40.133820, -75.980408
White Hall Mill	Caernarvon	Site	pre-1824	40.136295, -75.991816
Caernarvon Roller Mill	Caernarvon	Site	1868	40.138116, -75.988211
Weaver's Mill	Caernarvon	Site	1771	40.142415, -75.996137
Spring Grove Mill	East Earl	Business	1868	40.144343, -76.020204

Appendix C

Common Name	Township	Disposition	Built	Coordinates
Conestoga Roller Mill	East Earl	Site	late 1800s	40.142270, -76.031553
Linden Grove Mill	East Earl	Site	1851	40.140228, -76.048199
Greenville Mill	Earl	Business	1780	40.145978, -76.077974
Sensenig's Mill	Earl	Site	1875	40.149989, -76.093085
Keystone Mill	Earl	Site	1867	40.150681, -76.104335
Hinkletown Mill	Ephrata Township	Site	1797	40.153561, -76.127631
Eberly's Cider Mill (Bitzer's)	West Earl	Farm	1801	40.141148, -76.151158
East Earl Mill	East Earl	Site	1888	40.137751, -76.059147
Bitzer's Mill	West Earl	Site	1824	40.137526, -76.163681
Farmersville Mill	West Earl	Site	1872	40.135898, -76.172683
Brownstown Mill	West Earl	Residence	1856	40.127667, -76.199212
Earlville Mill	West Earl	Site	1889	40.120889, -76.213199
Graaf's Mill	West Earl	Site	1729	40.114732, -76.225663
H.E. Leaman Rifle Mills	Upper Leacock	Site	1834	40.106255, -76.247570
Bushong Mill (Zook's Flour Mill)	Upper Leacock	Active	1857	40.104606, -76.237205
Hunsecker's Mill	Manheim Township	Site	1800	40.088081, -76.248344

Appendix C

Common Name	Township	Disposition	Built	Coordinates
Binkley's Mill	Manheim Township	Site	1772	40.079094, -76.260031
Eden Roller Mill (Umble's)	East Lampeter	Storage	1870	40.070461, -76.261512
Twin Cities Mill	East Lampeter	Site	1763	40.044595, -76.273718
Twin City Mill	Lancaster Township	Site	1822	40.044059, -76.274622
Swarr's Mill (City Water Works)	Lancaster Township	Site	1803	40.033210, -76.280582
Neff's Mill (Old Factory Mill)	Lancaster City	Site	1728	40.022933, -76.284326
Engleside Mill	Lancaster Township	Site	1800	40.021902, -76.304654
Levan's Flour & Woolen Mill (Light's, Lock #1)	Lancaster Township	Site	1870	40.009989, -76.303305
Second Lock Mill (Haverstick's)	Pequea	Site	1815	40.003533, -76.313819
Wabank Mill (Lock #3)	Lancaster Township	Site	1807	39.998045, -76.329122
Slackwater Burr Mill (Shober's, Lock #4)	Conestoga	Site	1805	39.983623, -76.356899
Rockhill Mill (Mylin's)	Conestoga	Site	1870	39.961489, -76.364277
Kendig's Mill (Espenshade's, Lock #6)	Manor	Site	1818	39.951642, -76.368677

Appendix D

FLOODS

Floods recorded at Lancaster between 1933 and 2018

Rank	Date	Crest	Flow (cfs)	Category
1	6/23/1972	27.9	50,300	Major
2	9/8/2011	21.3	30,200	Major
3	1/25/1978	18.14	25,300	Major
4	10/9/2005	17.8	20,800	Major
5	8/24/1933	17.52	22,800	Major
6	9/9/1987	16.7	20,500	Major
7	9/17/1999	16.39	17,600	Major
8	5/6/1989	15.3	16,300	Major
9	5/23/1942	15.12	17,300	Major
10	6/28/2006	14.7	14,000	Moderate
11	7/28/2004	14.43	13,500	Moderate
12	8/4/2018	14.28	13,800	Moderate
13	10/30/2012	14.24	13,700	Moderate
14	6/17/1982	14.2	13,600	Moderate
15	3/22/2000	14.14	12,900	Moderate

Appendix D

Rank	Date	Crest	Flow (cfs)	Category
16	9/30/1934	14.04	15,000	Moderate
17	12/5/1993	13.95	12,600	Moderate
18	1/25/1979	13.91	13,000	Moderate
19	2/26/1979	13.87	12,900	Moderate
20	8/22/2018	13.86	13,000	Moderate
21	10/20/1996	13.22	11,200	Moderate
22	7/27/1986	13	11,000	Moderate
23	3/2/2007	12.95	10,700	Minor
24	7/7/1984	12.85	10,800	Minor
25	1/27/1976	12.84	12,600	Minor
26	7/8/1934	12.8	12,600	Minor
27	1/31/2013	12.77	11,000	Minor
28	9/23/2003	12.74	10,400	Minor
29	2/12/1985	12.71	10,600	Minor
30	6/2/1946	12.69	12,400	Minor
31	4/16/1983	12.48	10,200	Minor
32	1/20/1996	12.26	9,560	Minor
33	1/21/1979	12.25	9,830	Minor
34	8/28/2011	12.15	9,370	Minor
35	8/19/1955	12.11	11,200	Minor
36	5/19/1988	12.11	9,600	Minor
37	2/14/1971	12.08	11,200	Minor
38	7/22/1988	12	9,500	Minor
39	11/28/1993	11.95	9,060	Minor
40	12/13/1983	11.92	9,330	Minor
41	12/14/1996	11.9	9,000	Minor
42	5/1/2014	11.86	9,410	Minor
43	7/24/1988	11.8	9,200	Minor
44	9/13/1960	11.77	10,600	Minor

Appendix D

Rank	Date	Crest	Flow (cfs)	Category
45	3/27/1978	11.74	9,060	Minor
46	11/9/1996	11.7	8,700	Minor
47	6/21/2003	11.66	8,600	Minor
48	8/18/1942	11.6	10,300	Minor
49	6/29/1973	11.38	8,830	Minor
50	10/1/2010	11.35	8,180	Minor
51	10/11/2013	11.2	8,350	Minor
52	2/7/2004	11.09	7,815	Minor
53	11/17/2006	11.05	7,760	Minor

NOTES

Foreword

1. William Cronon, *Nature's Metropolis: Chicago and the Great West* (New York: W.W. Norton, 1991), 372.

Chapter 1

2. Ellis and Evans, *History of Lancaster County*, 10.
3. Ibid., 116.
4. Ruth, *The Earth Is the Lord's*, 117.
5. Merrell, *Into the American Woods*, 115.
6. Ruth, *The Earth Is the Lord's*, 120.
7. Ibid., 146.
8. Loose, *Heritage of Lancaster*, 6.
9. Ellis and Evans, *History of Lancaster County*, 26.
10. Brubaker, *Massacre of the Conestogas*, 134.

Chapter 2

11. Loose, *Heritage of Lancaster*, 12.
12. Frey, *Conestoga Wagon Lore*, 11.

13. Ellis and Evans, *History of Lancaster County*, 308.
14. Brubaker, *Remembering Lancaster County*, 34.
15. Hanson, "Henry E. Leman."
16. Laws of the Commonwealth of the Session 1835–36, no. 49, 135.
17. Loose, *Heritage of Lancaster*, 102.

Chapter 3

18. Brubaker, *Remembering Lancaster County*, 53.
19. Clark, "Early Conestoga Navigation," 317.
20. Ellis and Evans, *History of Lancaster County*, 317.
21. Clark, "Early Conestoga Navigation," 316
22. Schuleen, "Conestoga Navigation," 8.
23. Norris, "Report of a Committee of the Stockholders," 8.
24. Schuleen, "Conestoga Navigation," 8.
25. Norris, "Report of a Committee of the Stockholders," 9.
26. Schuleen, "Conestoga Navigation," 8.
27. Ellis and Evans, *History of Lancaster County*, 317.
28. Norris, "Report of a Committee of the Stockholders," 4.
29. An ark was a rough wooden craft made especially for river transport. They were typically sixteen to eighteen feet wide and about twenty-five feet long. Arks were made for one trip and were dismantled at the end of their journey, at which point the wood was sold.
30. Clark, "Early Conestoga Navigation," 325.
31. Ellis and Evans, *History of Lancaster County*, 318.
32. A packet boat was a medium-sized boat designed for mail, passenger and freight transportation. A typical canal packet could accommodate up to sixty persons.
33. Ellis and Evans, *History of Lancaster County*, 318.
34. Norris, "Report of a Committee of the Stockholders," 5.
35. Ibid., 6.
36. Clark, "Early Conestoga Navigation," 320.
37. Ellis and Evans, *History of Lancaster County*, 318.
38. Forney, "Voice of Lancaster," 12.
39. Riddle, *Story of Lancaster*, 215.
40. Ellis and Evans, *History of Lancaster County*, 518.
41. See also Smeltzer, *Canals Along the Lower Susquehanna*, 63.
42. Schuyler, "Other Blighted Residential Areas."

43. Forney, "Voice of Lancaster," 19.
44. Riddle, *Story of Lancaster*, 106.
45. Ellis and Evans, *History of Lancaster County*, 388.
46. Pennsylvania State Senate, "Edward Coleman."
47. Kline, "Lost Love of a Bachelor President."
48. Reninger, *Orange Street*, 54.
49. Ellis and Evans, *History of Lancaster County*, 316.

Chapter 4

50. Shumway, Durell and Frey, *Conestoga Wagon*, 18.
51. A Burr arch truss is a combination arch and kingpost design developed by Theodore Burr in 1804. The combination arch and truss results in a bridge that remains stable as a load is carried across the span.
52. Ellis and Evans, *History of Lancaster County*, 745.
53. Riddle, *Story of Lancaster*, 213–14.
54. Clark, "Early Conestoga Navigation," 323.
55. *American Miller*, 638.
56. Ellis and Evans, *History of Lancaster County*, 745.

Chapter 5

57. Diffenderffer, "Wabank House."
58. *Lancaster Sunday News*, August 16, 1925.
59. Water Supply Commission of Pennsylvania, "Water Resources Inventory Report," 82.
60. Ibid., 81.
61. Ibid., 83

Chapter 6

62. "Text of Engineer's Report," *Lancaster New Era*, January 3, 1920.
63. Rebman, *Conestoga River Watershed*, 8.
64. Ibid., 10.
65. Ibid., 21.
66. Moss and Kochel, *Journal of Geology*, 1.

67. Clare, *Brief History of Lancaster County*, 292.
68. Ad Crable, "The Woman Who Made Environmental History by Wading in the Polluted Conestoga River," Lancaster Newspapers, March 19, 2012.

Chapter 7

69. Schuyler, "Myth, Memory, and the Meaning of Community," 614–38.

SOURCES

American Miller 41 (August 1913).
Brubaker, Jack. *Massacre of the Conestogas*. Charleston, SC: The History Press, 2010.
———. *Remembering Lancaster County*. Charleston, SC: The History Press, 2010.
———. "The Tragic Story of Another Coleman Suitor." Lancaster Online, March 4, 2016. lancasteronline.com/opinion/columnists/the-tragic-story-of-another-coleman-suitor/article_b9774974-e175-11e5-ad8e-47a1cb892918.html.
Clare, Israel Smith. *A Brief History of Lancaster County*. N.p.: Argus Publishing Company, 1891.
Clark, Martha Bladen. "Early Conestoga Navigation." *Journal of the Lancaster County Historical Society* 12, no. 9.
Diffenderffer, Frank Reid. "The Wabank House: The Story of a Lancaster County Resort." *Journal of the Lancaster County Historical Society* (1904–05).
Ellis, Franklin, and Samuel Evans. *History of Lancaster County, Pennsylvania*. N.p.: Everts & Peck, 1883.
Eshleman, George Ross. *The Lancaster Law Review*. Vol. 37, 1920–21. Lancaster, PA: Wickersham Printing Company, 1921.
Floodplain Restoration Book. Lititz, PA: Land Studies Inc., 2007.
Forney, J.W. "The Voice of Lancaster on the Subject of a National Foundry." Report to U.S. Congress, 1839.

Sources

Frey, H.C. *Conestoga Wagon Lore.* N.p.: Pennsylvania Dutch Folklore Center, Inc., 1951.

Hanson, Charles E., Jr. "Henry E. Leman, Riflemaker." *American Society of Arms Collectors* 51 (1984).

Holzinger, Philip R. *50 Ways to Save Lancaster County.* Lancaster, PA: self-published, 1996.

Kline, Philip S. "The Lost Love of a Bachelor President." *American Heritage Magazine.* www.americanheritage.com/lost-love-bachelor-president.

Loose, John Ward Willson. *The Heritage of Lancaster.* N.p.: Windsor Publications, Inc., 1978.

Lord, Arthur C. *Water-Powered Grist Mills, Lancaster County, Pennsylvania.* Self-published, 1996.

Merrell, James H. *Into the American Woods: Negotiators on the Pennsylvania Frontier.* New York: W.W. Norton & Co., 1999.

Moss, John H., and R. Craig Kochel. *The Journal of Geology.* Chicago: Chicago Press, 1978.

Norris, William. "Report of a Committee of the Stockholders of the Conestogo Navigation Company." 1832.

Pennsylvania State Senate, Historical Biographies. "Edward Coleman." www.legis.state.pa.us/cfdocs/legis/BiosHistory/MemBio.cfm?ID=4458&body=S).

Rebman, Earl. *Conestoga Watershed: Outline of History, 1710–1973.* Self-published, 1973.

Reninger, Marion W. *Orange Street.* Lancaster, PA, 1954.

Riddle, William. *The Story of Lancaster: Old and New.* Lancaster, PA: self-published, 1917.

Ruth, John Landis. *The Earth Is the Lord's.* N.p.: Herald Press, 2001.

Schuleen, Ernest T., comp. "Conestoga Navigation, A Collection of Pertinent Data." Lancaster County Historical Society, 1983.

Schuyler, David. "Myth, Memory, and the Meaning of Community: Sunnyside (Lancaster, Pennsylvania) and the Limits of Planning." *Proceedings of the American Philosophical Society* 142, no. 4 (1998): 614–38. www.jstor.org/stable/3152285.

———. "Other Blighted Residential Areas." Franklin and Marshall College. https://www.fandm.edu/david-schuyler/changing-face-of-lancaster/other-blighted-residential-areas.

Shumway, George, Edward Durell and Howard Frey. *Conestoga Wagon, 1750–1850.* N.p.: self-published, 1966.

Smeltzer, Gerald. *Canals Along the Lower Susquehanna.* York, PA: Historical Society of York County, 1963.

SOURCES

Water Supply Commission of Pennsylvania. "Water Resources Inventory Report." Harrisburg, PA, 1917, 82.

Wood, Jerome H., Jr. *Conestoga Crossroads, Lancaster, Pennsylvania, 1730–1790.* N.p.: Pennsylvania Historical and Museum Commission, 1979.

ABOUT THE AUTHOR

Donald Kautz was born, grew up and still lives in the Conestoga Valley. He graduated from Conestoga Valley High School during the torrential downpour of Hurricane Agnes in 1972. Don lives with his wife, Mary Beth, in a suburb of Lancaster City about one mile from the Conestoga River. They have three grown children. Don is a software developer by avocation and an avid photographer as a hobby. More of Don's photography may be viewed on his website at www.dlkautzphoto.com.

www.ingramcontent.com/pod-product-compliance
Lightning Source LLC
Chambersburg PA
CBHW070356100426
42812CB00005B/1525